IELTS

Preparation and Practice

Reading and Writing
ACADEMIC MODULE

Wendy Sahanaya
Jeremy Lindeck
Richard Stewart

INDONESIA AUSTRALIA LANGUAGE FOUNDATION

OXFORD
UNIVERSITY PRESS

OXFORD

UNIVERSITY PRESS

253 Normanby Road, South Melbourne, Victoria 3205, Australia

Oxford University Press is a department of the University of Oxford.
It furthers the University's objective of excellence in research, scholarship,
and education by publishing worldwide in
Oxford New York

Auckland   Cape Town   Dar es Salaam   Hong Kong   Karachi
Kuala Lumpur   Madrid   Melbourne   Mexico City   Nairobi
New Delhi   Shanghai   Taipei   Toronto

With offices in

Argentina   Austria   Brazil   Chile   Czech Republic   France   Greece
Guatemala   Hungary   Italy   Japan   Poland   Portugal   Singapore
South Korea   Switzerland   Thailand   Turkey   Ukraine   Vietnam

OXFORD is a trade mark of Oxford University Press
in the UK and in certain other countries

National Library of Australia
Cataloguing-in-Publication data:

Sahanaya, Wendy. 1940–.
IELTS preparation and practice: reading and writing:
academic module.

ISBN 0 19 554093 X.
ISBN 978 0 19 554093 2.

1. English language – Examinations. 2. International English
Language Testing System. 3. English language –
Examinations, questions, etc. I. Title. II. Title:
International English Language Testing System preparation
and practice. (Series: IELTS preparation and practice).

428

Typeset by Stephen Chan
Printed in China by Golden Cup Printing Co.,Ltd

Contents

Preface

How to Use this Book

There are two main sections to this book: the reading and the writing. The *Practice tests* and the *exercises* have been numbered separately in each section. Answers for the exercises and the Practice tests are in the *Answer Key* at the end of the book.

Section 1   Reading

Section 1 gives you:
- an overview of the test which describes the Academic Reading, the form of the instructions and the question types.
- a Practice Reading test. You should do this test giving yourself exactly one hour.
- the question types in detail. For each question type there is an *Explanation* at the beginning. The purpose of this explanation is to help you understand the purpose of the question type and learn the appropriate skill for answering the question. After the explanation, there is a *Practice and Discussion* section. Here useful skills and strategies will be explained in detail. Then there are exercises for you to practise the skills. Follow the instructions for each activity and, when you have finished, check your answers in the Answer Key. Because working fast and efficiently is very important in tests, many exercises have a *Time target*. The Time target gives you a suggested time limit for the activity.
- two Practice Reading tests.

Section 2   Writing

Section 2 begins with an overview of the Writing test and the instructions then describes in detail the two Writing tasks.

You can do the sections in any sequence you wish.

The Reading Test

About the Reading Test

The IELTS Academic Reading test takes 60 minutes.

There is a question booklet which contains all the instructions, the reading passages and the questions.

There is an answer sheet (on the back of the Listening test answer sheet). You **must** put all your answers on the answer sheet while you are reading. There is no time allowed at the end for transferring answers.

The test is divided into three sections. Each section is more difficult than the one before. Each reading passage is between 700 and 1000 words long.

There are between 38 and 42 questions. The questions may come **before** or **after** the readings. There is a variety of possible question types. There may be examples of how to answer the questions. There is a more detailed explanation of the questions later in the book.

You may mark or write on the question paper, but all answers must be written on the answer sheet. Remember you must write your answers on the answer sheet **as you go**. Unlike in the Listening test, there is no time to transfer them at the end of the test.

Getting the Instructions Right

The written instructions in the reading booklet are always given in *italics*. Important aspects of the instructions are also in ***BOLD ITALIC CAPITALS***.

The instructions in the Reading test depend on the type of question. As you work through this book, take particular note of instructions. Getting to know the instructions now means that you will be able to see quickly what you have to do in the actual test and will be less likely to make the more common mistakes.

Following are seven examples of instructions which are typical of those you will find in the IELTS Academic Reading booklet. Read each of the instructions below and the explanations that follow.

EXAMPLE 1

Questions 1–5

*Choose the appropriate letters **A–D** and write them in boxes 1–5 on your answer sheet.*

This instruction typically applies to multiple-choice questions. One of the answers – **A, B, C** or **D** – will be the correct answer.

EXAMPLE 2

Questions 11–15

*Reading Passage 2 has five sections **A–E**. Choose the most suitable heading for each section from the list of headings below. Write the appropriate numbers (i–ix) in boxes 11–15 on your answer sheet.*

Note: *There are more headings than sections so you will not use all of them. You may use any heading more than once.*

This means the sections are given the headings **A, B, C, D** and **E.** The answer choices, (i.e. the headings) usually appear in a box and will be numbered using roman numerals. You will write those roman numerals on your answer sheet.

There are always extra headings. Although you are told 'You may use any heading more than once.' you will rarely need to do so.

There can be a question of this type asking for a heading for only one paragraph or a heading for the whole passage.

Often there will be an example given. It is unlikely this example will be used again.

EXAMPLE 3

Questions 11–15

*Choose **ONE** phrase **A–F** from the list to complete each key point. Write the appropriate letters **A–F** in boxes 11–15 on your answer sheet.*

The information in the completed sentences should be an accurate summary of points made by the writer.

Note: *There are more phrases **A–F** than sentences so you will not use them all. You may use any phrase more than once.*

This is like the headings instruction. Usually you will have to match the first half of a sentence with the second half. The completed sentences will always be paraphrases or summaries of information in the text.

A similar instruction could ask you to match lists of points such as causes and effects, or advantages and disadvantages.

It is possible that you will use a phrase more than once.

EXAMPLE 4

Questions 12–15

Look at Questions 12–15. Classify the following as linked in the passage to:

M *Mammals*
B *Birds*
F *Fish*

*Write the appropriate letters **M**, **B** or **F** in boxes 12–15 on your answer sheet.*

Again this is rather like the headings instruction. You classify the points given in each question to the appropriate category in the list.

EXAMPLE 5

Questions 22–27

a *Using **NO MORE THAN THREE WORDS**, answer the following questions. Write your answers in boxes 22–27.*

OR

b *Complete the sentence(s) below with words taken from Reading Passage 3. Use **NO MORE THAN THREE WORDS** for each answer. Write your answers in boxes 22–27.*

OR

c *Complete the table [notes/summary] below. Choose **ONE or TWO WORDS** from the passage for each answer. Write your answers in boxes 22–27.*

There are two key points you will always need to check with this instruction type:
• **the number of words** you should use for your answer
• **where** the words come from: the passage or your own words.

EXAMPLE 6

Questions 25–31

Do the following statements agree with the views of [summarise the opinions of/reflect the attitudes of] the writer in Reading Passage 1?

In boxes 25–31 on your answer sheet write:

 YES *if the statement agrees with the writer*

 NO *if the statement contradicts the writer*

 NOT GIVEN *if it is impossible to say what the writer thinks about this.*

For your answers to questions with an instruction like this you may also write:

- **Y** instead of **YES**
- **N** instead of **NO** and
- **NG** instead of **NOT GIVEN**.

EXAMPLE 7

Questions 33–40

a *Complete the notes [summary/diagram] below. Choose your answers [labels] from the box below the notes [summary/diagram] and write them in boxes 33–40 on your answer sheet.*

Note: *There are more words [labels] than spaces so you will not use them all. You may use any of the words more than once.*

OR

b *Complete the summary of the main ideas in Reading Passage 2. Choose **ONE** or **TWO WORDS** from the passage for each answer. Write your answers in boxes 25–31 on your answer sheet.*

OR

c *Complete the summary below of the main ideas in Section B on page 5. Choose your answers from the box below the summary and write them in boxes 25–31 on your answer sheet.*

Note: *There are more words than spaces so you will not use them all. You may use any of the words more than once.*

These instructions could apply to a set of notes, a summary or a diagram based on information in the reading passage. The important points for you to note are:

- **the number of words** you should use for your answer
- **where** the words come from: the passage or the words given in a box.

You might have to use the same word or phrase more than once.

Make a copy of the blank Reading answer sheet at the end of the book and do this Practice test.

Note: There is no separate answer key for this test. You will find the answers as you work through the exercises in the rest of the book.

IELTS PRACTICE TEST 1

READING

TIME ALLOWED: 1 hour

NUMBER OF QUESTIONS: 39

Instructions

All answers must be written on the answer sheet

The test is divided as follows:

Reading Passage 1	*Questions 1–13*
Reading Passage 2	*Questions 14–25*
Reading Passage 3	*Questions 26–39*

Start at the beginning of the test and work through it. You should answer all the questions.

If you cannot do a particular question leave it and go on to the next. You can return to it later.

READING PASSAGE 1

You should spend about 20 minutes on Questions 1–13 which are based on Reading Passage 1 on pages 2 and 3.

RELIGIOUS DENTISTRY

Bali is, without doubt, one of the most culturally rich islands in the world. In fact, its carved temples, dances and immaculately manicured rice terraces do all seem too perfect to be true, even down to the people's smiles. But take a closer look at those smiles and the perfect teeth do seem a bit too perfect, and for good reason. Those flattened teeth are the result of an important piece of dentistry that every young Balinese man or woman experiences in their life, known as *potong gigi*, or tooth filing.

Tooth filing is part of Bali's religious traditions and is not performed for cosmetic reasons. In fact, so important is the tooth filing ceremony that without it, the Balinese believe they may experience serious social or behavioural problems later in life, or their personality may change altogether.

Balinese religious life is surrounded by a belief in a variety of deities – gods and demons that inhabit different levels of the cosmic and real worlds. These deities range from the most holy in the mountains to the lowest that inhabit the ground and the sea. There are gods and goddesses in every walk of life which have special forces of their own. They inhabit temple statues, trees, even fly through the air. They exist together in a dual concept of good and evil, clean and dirty, etc. As such, both the good and the evil spirits must be appeased, and offerings are thus made at the myriad temples on the island.

It is not only the good spirits that are worshipped, for Bali has a dark and evil side too. Terrifying demons and monsters walk the earth and although they are seldom seen, they too must be appeased. These demons can take over and inhabit the body of an animal or human and wreak havoc in the community, so it is very important to strike a balance between offerings made to all spirits that swarm the island. At every stage in a person's life, he or she is susceptible to influences of the supernatural — from demons and *layak*, to good spirits which may bring luck. Purification of the body and mind is therefore central to Balinese religious life and the tooth-filing ceremony represents one such rite of passage from childhood to becoming an adult.

According to the Balinese, long pointed teeth resemble the fangs of animals and these give the person characteristics of the animal sides of human nature and ferocity. The Balinese believe there are six of these evil qualities: desire, greed, anger, intoxication, irresoluteness and jealousy. These are liable to flare up, along with animal instincts, when the canines are still sharp. To prevent this, the points of the canines are filed down, together with any prominent points of the lower teeth in a special *potong gigi* ceremony. Although this may prevent the person taking on animal instincts and beautify the smile, it is, unfortunately offset by early tooth decay since the protective enamel is removed from the points of the teeth, exposing them to acid decay. The situation is exacerbated in those who go on to chew betel nuts, since the caustic lime rapidly attacks the teeth.

The *potong gigi* ceremony usually is undertaken for members of the same family together since it is a very expensive occasion to host. It is often necessary to wait until the youngest child is of age. Girls are ready for tooth filing only when they have reached sexual maturity and boys are usually older, about 17 or at least after puberty. A person must have their teeth filed before marriage and since marriage is early, the ceremony is often undertaken as a pre-nuptial event.

The high priest is consulted first to choose an auspicious day from the Balinese calendar. Every day has a different function – a best day for rice planting, best day for cremations and other festivals, as well as tooth-filing days. The dentist's chair, so to speak, is specially constructed for the ceremony from bamboo in the form of a rack covered with coconut leaves, blankets and a variety of offerings and frangipani flowers. Surrounding the platform is food for the guests and a huge display of skewered suckling pig, fruit, and whole roasted chickens adorn the entrance to the ceremony room.

Questions 1–6

*Choose the appropriate letters **A–D** and write them in boxes 1–6 on your answer sheet.*

1 The Balinese have their teeth filed

    A to have a perfect smile

    B for cosmetic reasons

    C to avoid problems in life

    D to change their personality

2 Balinese spirits

    A are usually easily seen

    B are only found in the mountains

    C can all fly through the air

    D can be found anywhere

3 *Layak* are probably

    A good spirits

    B evil spirits

    C tooth-filing experts

    D people whose teeth have been filed

4 When do many Balinese have their teeth filed?

    A just before getting married   **B** as part of the marriage ceremony

    C in early childhood   **D** when the high priest has time

5 Where does tooth filing take place?

    A in the dentist's surgery   **B** at the village temple

    C on a special platform   **D** in the family residence

6 What is the most likely source of this passage?

    A an undergraduate essay   **B** a scientific journal

    C a current affairs news magazine   **D** an airline magazine

Questions 7–13

Do the following statements agree with the views of the writer in Reading Passage 1?

In boxes 7–13 on your answer sheet write:

    YES *if the statement agrees with the writer*

    NO *if the statement contradicts the writer*

    NOT GIVEN *if it is impossible to say what the writer thinks about this*

  7 Most Balinese are nervous about having their teeth filed.

  8 Only the canine teeth are filed down.

  9 Tooth decay soon occurs in the filed teeth.

10 Balinese religious tradition is rich and varied.

11 The tooth filing is done by the high priest.

12 There is a feast after the filing has been done.

13 Balinese custom does not permit the filing to be done for more than one person at a time.

READING PASSAGE 2

You should spend about 20 minutes on Questions 14–25 which are based on Reading Passage 2 on pages 6 and 7.

Reading Passage 2 has 6 sections A–F.

Questions 14–18

*From the list of headings below choose the most suitable heading for sections **A–F**.*

*Write the appropriate numbers (**i–ix**) in boxes 14–18 on your answer sheet.*

Note: *There are more headings than sections so you will not use all of them. You may use any of the headings more than once.*

HEADINGS

(i)	Increasing popularity of pets in Australia
(ii)	Dogs in cities
(iii)	Benefits of pet ownership
(iv)	Pet ownership in Australia
(v)	Private open space and landscaping
(vi)	Criticisms of pet ownership in Australian cities
(vii)	Keeping pets under control
(viii)	Pet owners' obligations
(ix)	Housing and precinct design
(x)	Pet research

Example	Answer
Section E	**ix**

---

14 Section A

15 Section B

16 Section C

17 Section D

18 Section F

DOMESTIC PETS IN NEW URBAN AREAS

The role of urban design in successful pet ownership

This paper summarises the findings of an investigation into the role of urban design in successful pet ownership. There are several reasons why planners should consider pets in decisions about residential and open space development.

A People are not generally aware of the popularity of pet ownership in Australia. The Morgan Research surveys estimate that in 1992, 37% of Australian households owned one or more dogs, and 30% owned one or more cats. Fifty-three per cent of all households owned either a dog or a cat. Pet-owning households are clearly a substantial group within the community.

B Research shows that pets play an important role in teaching children about sharing, caring, communication and responsibility. They also act as companions and protectors, stress relievers and in some cases help to foster family cohesion. While pets are traditionally associated with family-type households, they are just as important to households without children; indeed they are often surrogates for children in childless families. This applies particularly to the elderly, who usually form very close associations with their pets. In an era when the population is ageing and more people are living alone, pets can provide valuable relief from loneliness.

C Urban pet management has been the subject of extensive debate among veterinarians and those involved in local government for some time. Part of the reason is that people complain more readily about other people's pets than ever before. Emphasis on urban consol-idation has meant that smaller homes and back gardens and multi-dwelling developments not only discourage people from owning pets but also place greater demands on scarce public open space. Pet owners may face tougher restrictions from either their local council or resident management committee.

D The term *socially responsible pet ownership* has emerged to describe a set of responsibilities to which pet owners are now expected to adhere. In meeting their responsibilities pet owners need to consider:

■ Providing an enriching environment to reduce unwanted behaviour; e.g. excessive barking.

■ Confining dogs to their premises. The advantages of this include protection from catching disease, being run over and fighting. Ideally cats should be confined to the house at night for their own protection where practicable.

■ Training pets to alter unacceptable behaviour.

■ Exercising dogs, especially if they spend long periods on their own.

E It might be tempting to prescribe different pets for different types of housing. Some people already have firm views about pets and housing type, mostly in relation to dogs, e.g. that the only environment for a dog is in conventional detached housing or that a "big" dog is only suitable in the country. However, suitability is as much dependent on the quality of space as it is on the quantity.

A dwelling that overlooks areas of activity is ideal for pets because it increases the amount of stimulation that can be received from the property, e.g. dwellings that overlook a park or are adjacent to a busy street. This is one way to alleviate boredom and the negative behaviours that sometimes result.

Preferably a dog should have access to some outdoor space. Open space is not essential for a cat provided an enriching environment is maintained indoors, e.g. a bay window or internal fernery. Ideally dogs should have access to all areas of open space on a property. On the whole a dog's behaviour is likely to be better if he or she can see the street. Although the dog may bark at passers-by in the street, there will be less likelihood of excessive barking that might arise through boredom. Providing a dog with surveillance of the street also enhances public security – a very positive benefit.

F   With adequate fencing, a dog will be confined to the property. Cats are less easily constrained and are discussed below. The standard paling fence will restrain almost all dogs. They are recommended for side and rear boundaries. Solid front fences limit the view of the outside world and are not recommended. The dog will tend to be less roused by sound stimuli if he or she can see passers-by or activities in the street. However, it is important to ensure that the dog cannot get through the fence. Furthermore, all gates should be fitted with a return spring self-closing device.

Cats are not as easily restrained as dogs as they are more agile and have quite different notions of territoriality. Mostly this does not create a problem, although difficulties may arise in environmentally sensitive areas where cats may prey on wildlife. It is recommended that cats be confined to the house at night for their own protection.

The pleasures and benefits of pet ownership should be available to everyone. However, owning a pet brings with it responsibilities to which we are increasingly being called to adhere. It is hoped that the guidelines will encourage people to think about pets in decisions about residential and community development. If they do, pet ownership will not be prejudiced by the push for urban consolidation.

Questions 19–24

Do the following statements reflect the claims of the writer of Reading Passage 2?

In boxes 19–24 on your answer sheet write:

> **YES**   *if the statement agrees with the writer*
>
> **NO**   *if the statement contradicts the writer*
>
> **NOT GIVEN**   *if there is no information about this in the passage*

19   Research shows that more than half of Australian families have both a cat and a dog.

20   Many pets get lonely when their owners are away from home.

21   Although having outdoor space available is good for cats and dogs, it is not absolutely essential.

22   While fences are good for keeping animals off the streets, they should not block the animal's view of street activities.

23   Dogs should be encouraged to bark at everybody going by.

24   It is safer for cats if they are kept in the house at night.

Question 25

*Which of the following statements **A–D** best reflects the views of the writer of Reading Passage 2?*

*Choose the appropriate letter **A–D** and write it in box 25 on your answer sheet.*

A   Although many people keep dogs in the city, this is not truly a suitable environment for them.

B   Although the city is less satisfactory than the country for keeping pets, it is still recommended that families with children and older people have a pet of some kind.

C   Keeping pets in cities is appropriate so long as the owners ensure they do not annoy others.

D   Having a pet in the city can be a rewarding experience for all concerned provided sensible precautions are taken to ensure the pet has a satisfactory environment.

READING PASSAGE 3

You should spend about 20 minutes on Questions 26–39 which are based on Reading Passage 3 on pages 9 and 10.

Australian Mining Companies In The Asia-Pacific Region

Environmental impact on people

Mining operations by their very nature have major impacts, positive and negative, on the local area and on local communities. They are usually in remote places and the people affected are often isolated or neglected communities.

It is inevitable that mining operations will disturb the environment in a fairly dramatic way. Forest cover may have to be cut down to clear the site of the mine or for access roads. Tunnels or open-cut pits are dug. Overburden* is removed and dumped nearby, usually to erode slowly into nearby streams and rivers. Tailings** from the ore processing plant have to be put somewhere – preferably into an on-site tailings dam, but more likely straight into a river and/or the sea.

Mine tailings may contain some dangerous chemicals, but the major problem is usually the huge amounts of solid sediment that they put into the river system, and the effect this has on water quality and marine life. This can directly affect the livelihood of people living downstream who depend on the river for fish, for drinking water for themselves and their animals, or for cooking or washing. Heavy sedimentation can silt up rivers, making transportation difficult and causing fields and forests by the river banks to flood.

Other environmental effects can include air pollution from trucks tearing along dusty access roads, or more seriously, fumes from ore processing plants. Kelera, a woman who lives with her husband and two school-age children near the Australian-owned Emperor Gold Mine in Fiji, describes it thus:

When the gas comes, sometimes in the morning, if falls like a mist, and all the children start coughing, and we cough too. The people who get asthma, they are the ones who are really frightened to death. But what can you do? When the gas comes you have to breathe it… You know how strong it is? I tell you. The chili and the betel leaves that we grow, they just die. It's as though you took hot water and spilled it on the grass, and the next day you go and see what it looks like. It's just like that.

Social impact

The social impact of a modern mining operation in a remote area can also be great. Some people may have to move

---

*Overburden – worthless rock or soil covering valuable ore

**Tailings – waste rock or ore from a mining operation

off their land to make way for the mine. Many more will probably relocate themselves voluntarily, moving in from more remote areas to the mining road or the mining settlement, drawn by the prospects of jobs and money, trade stores and health clinics, or just by the general excitement of the place. In many cases the men will come in by themselves, leaving the women to fend for themselves back in the village. Traditional agriculture and other pursuits are, as a result, often neglected.

But the social environment into which they come is a culturally alien one which can undermine traditional kin and gender relations and traditional authority and control, often with bitter consequences.

Large amounts of cash will normally be injected into the local community in the form of royalties or compensation to landowners, wages to mine workers or payments to sub-contractors. While this can be very beneficial it can also lead to inequalities, disputes and problems.

Those in the local community who acquire cash from wages or compensation and the power that goes with it are not necessarily those who by tradition hold power in that society. The very advent of the cash can have a disruptive effect on traditional social structures.

Also in societies where resources including cash are owned communally and shared out according to traditional rules and precedents, the injection of very large amounts of money can strain the rules and tempt some to keep more than their entitlement, thus causing internal rifts, disputes and fighting.

Disputes between landowners and mining companies over payments or compensation are also common, and can lead to violent reactions against landowners by the police or armed forces, or repression by the authorities.

For and against

Mining also, of course, brings considerable benefits. Locally it provides jobs and incomes, and for those who use their income wisely, an escape from grinding poverty and a life of hardship and struggle. It also brings development and services such as roads, wharfs, airstrips, stores, health clinics and schools, to areas which are usually remote and often neglected by government. The advent of health care and educational facilities to remote areas that would otherwise not have them can be especially beneficial.

Opinions about a mine will usually vary. Those most in favour tend to be those living near the mine and enjoying its facilities, who have been generously compensated for loss of land or damaged environment, or who are earning good money as mine workers or sub-contractors. Among those least in favour will be women living in or near the mining settlements who have to put up with alcoholism, domestic violence, sexual harassment or other social ills, and people living downstream, far enough away from the mine to be receiving little or no compensation but who nevertheless suffer its polluting effects.

Questions 26–31

*Using **NO MORE THAN THREE WORDS**, answer the following questions which are based on the first part of Reading Passage 3, 'Environmental impact on people'.*

Write your answers in boxes 26–31 on your answer sheet.

26 In what kind of areas do mining operations usually occur?

27 What will be cleared from a site before mining begins?

28 Where do the tailings come from?

29 What aspect of mining will have the major impact on the river system?

30 What two air pollutants are often associated with a mining operation?

31 What does the overburden consist of?

Questions 32–39

Complete the summary below which is based on the second part of Reading Passage 3, 'Social impact'. Choose your answers from the box below the summary and write them in boxes 32–39 on your answer sheet.

Note: *There are more words than spaces so you will not use them all. You may use any of the words more than once.*

SUMMARY

Once a mining operation begins the ..**(32)**.. is likely to change considerably. Many people will leave the area, and not all will go ..**(33)**.. Most outsiders who come into the area will find ..**(34)**.. in a culturally alien social environment. Among local villagers there will often be changes in the traditional ..**(35)**.. which may create dissension. There will also often be ..**(36)**.. over land. Often the intervention of the ..**(37)**.. will be necessary to settle them. All of these factors can have a disastrous ..**(38)**.. on the society.

However, improvements in infrastructure and in the provision of ..**(39)**.. services will be beneficial for the community.

power structure	health and education	disputes
themselves	authorities	local population
voluntarily	away	impact
local people	factors	outsiders
consideration	wharfs and airstrips	development

The Question Types

There are four main question types in the Academic Reading Module. These are:
- overview questions
- specific information questions
- viewpoint questions
- summarising questions.

Overview questions

These questions will often require you to choose a heading for different sections of the reading. You will be given a number of possible headings to choose from. There are always more headings than you will need. You will not always have to give a heading to every section. Sometimes these questions will be multiple-choice questions asking you what the topic of a particular section is.

Specific information questions

These questions could take several forms. The most common are:
- multiple-choice
- questions requiring a short answer
- completing sentences
- matching lists of items
- classifying items.

Viewpoint questions

The most common form for this question requires you to identify whether statements agree with the views or claims of the writer or of other people mentioned in the reading.

There could also be multiple-choice questions about the writer's attitude.

Summarising questions

The most common form for this type of question requires you to complete a short summary of information contained in the reading. You could also be asked to match two phrases or two parts of a sentence to summarise some of the information contained in the passage. You may also have to choose a title for the whole passage, usually one of four answer choices.

Each of these question types will be illustrated and practised in detail in the relevant sections which follow. Any question type can occur with any reading.

Overview Questions

For **each section** of the Reading test, the best strategy is to read **all** instructions, questions and examples very quickly. This gives you a clear focus when you read the passage and helps you to decide the best strategy for dealing with the questions.

If there are overview questions which require you to match headings with sections of the text, they always come before the reading. If there are questions which require you to choose the best topic from several options, they come after the reading. In both cases the best strategy is to quickly skim the passage.

- Read the first sentence of each paragraph.
- Skim the rest of each paragraph looking for key words.
- Match the headings with the sections.
- Write the heading numbers beside the appropriate sections in the test booklet.
- Read the text more closely to confirm your choices.

Practice

The following exercise will give you practice with this strategy.

Only the first sentence of each paragraph is given.

- Read the instructions.
- Read the headings.
- Read the first sentence of each paragraph once.
- Assign one or more headings to each section as you read.

Time target – 5 minutes

Questions 1–4

*The following Reading Passage has six sections A–F. Choose the most suitable heading for the sections from the list of headings below. Write the appropriate numbers (**i–viii**) in boxes 1–4 on your answer sheet.*

Note: *There are more headings than sections so you will not use all of them. You may use any of the headings more than once.*

HEADINGS

(i) Accommodating newcomers

(ii) World Bank efforts

(iii) Community participation

(iv) Upgrading housing

(v) Community leaders

(vi) Better infrastructure

(vii) Getting business involved

(viii) New regeneration strategies

---

1 Section C

2 Section D

3 Section E

4 Section F

READING PASSAGE

URBAN REGENERATION

A The science-fiction city of the future – Le Corbusier's grand schemes, or Niemeyer's Brasilia – seems ever less likely to replace our decaying cities and sprawling slums. A few new "open field" towns may be built as satellites to our biggest cities to fulfill this dream but will not house the urban poor. The new urban strategies are aimed at mobilising local communities and stretching scarce resources to cope with massive problems.

B The massive slum clearance and building boom of the '60s and '70s are over and reaction has set in.

C Community involvement and leadership are critical… Encouraging a dialogue between city officials and shantytown dwellers can produce more effective initiative than top-down planning.

D Current thinking aims at providing incentives to employers, through aid and technical advice, and the provision of small workshops.

E The World Bank has funded improvement schemes worldwide.

In the last decade "sites and services" schemes have concentrated on providing water, sanitation, street foundations and power, but left construction of housing to individual occupants.

F Whenever cityward migrations have reached unusual proportions, conventional housing and infrastructure services have been hard-pressed to cope.

DISCUSSION

You already know that heading viii has been used in the example. Therefore, it will probably not be used again.

You do not have to choose a heading for section B, even though it has been given a section letter. The IELTS does not always require you to choose a heading for every section. Check this before answering the questions.

Section C (Question 1)

In the first sentence in Section C, there are two key words that match two of the answer choices. These are *community* and *leadership*. Also, the word *involvement* is a synonym of *participation*. Therefore, at this stage, you would write in your question booklet **iii** and **v**. If you look at the first sentence of the second paragraph in this section, you find several other key words which indicate that your choices are on the right track. Can you find any clues that might help you decide which of these two is the correct choice?

Section D (Question 2)

This time there are no words the same as the words in the answer choices. However, there are close synonyms which indicate that choice **vii** might be the answer here. These are the words *business* and *employers*.

Section E (Question 3)

The first sentence and answer choice **ii** both mention the World Bank. But when you read the first sentence of the second paragraph you see that services, such as water, sanitation, street foundations and power are mentioned. These are all types of infrastructure. So you must also consider answer choice **vi** for this section.

Section F (Question 4)

This sentence talks about *cityward migrations*. People coming to the city are newcomers. But *housing* is also mentioned in this sentence as well as in answer choice **iv**. Answer choice **i** mentions *accommodating newcomers*, which includes housing.

So in an IELTS test you would write **in your question book**: iii and v beside Section C, **vii** beside Section D, **ii** and **vi** beside Section E, and **i** and **iv** beside Section F. Now you will have to read the passage in greater detail to confirm your choices and make your final selections.

However, in the real IELTS you cannot spend your time reading the complete passage in order to confirm a few answers. You need to keep other questions on that passage in mind at the same time. As you are reading, you should mark sections of the reading passage that might provide answers to these questions.

Look at some other questions for this same passage before you begin reading.

Questions 5–9.

*Choose the appropriate letter **A–C**.*

5 Le Corbusier and Niemeyer are probably

  A traffic engineers

  B architects

  C builders

6 El Salvador is given as an example of a country which

  A is decaying

  B experienced civil unrest

  C operated a community self-help scheme

7 What percentage of the economy of a large city in a developing country is likely to be found in the informal sector?

  A 30

  B 40–60

  C 60–80

8 Which scheme is given as an example of one making improvements with World Bank funding?

  A El Salvador

  B Lusaka

  C Francistown

9 In order to limit the number of people migrating to cities the author suggests that governments should

  A invest more in rural areas

  B provide better water supplies

  C let settlers build their own houses

Now read the complete passage that follows to confirm your answers to Questions 1–4 and to answer Questions 5–9.

URBAN REGENERATION

A The science-fiction city of the future – Le Corbusier's grand schemes, or Niemeyer's Brasilia – seems ever less likely to replace our decaying cities and sprawling slums. A few new "open field" towns may be built as satellites to our biggest cities to fulfill this dream but will not house the urban poor. The new urban strategies are aimed at mobilising local communities and stretching scarce resources to cope with massive problems.

B The massive slum clearance and building boom of the '60s and '70s are over and reaction has set in. The human costs of uprooting communities, to re-house them in socially and constructionally disastrous high-rise blocks, are all too evident. Gradual renewal of our decaying city centres is now under way, through reuse of existing structures plus more sensitive new architecture. The renewal is often community-based and many small agencies have sprung up to help municipal and private efforts. Nothing, however, can replace major long-term investment by governments to deal with obsolescence and disrepair.

C Community involvement and leadership are critical. El Salvador, prior to heightened civil unrest in the early '80s, boasted an almost model scheme – a local non-profit making group concentrating on low-cost housing, operating through long-term repayment, appropriate technology and communal self-help.

Encouraging a dialogue between city officials and shantytown dwellers can produce more effective initiative than top-down planning. Redirected, local skills and organisation can carry out low-cost schemes on a large scale, as in El Salvador. Establishing local administrative centres helps to focus community spirit, and allows a degree of self-management.

D Current thinking aims at providing incentives to employers, through aid and technical advice, and the provision of small workshops. The World Bank now funds many such schemes. The huge informal economy of many large cities (between 40% and 60% in Jakarta, Bombay and Lima, for example) is a major provider of jobs, and at present receives negligible support through government credit.

E The World Bank has funded improvement schemes worldwide. They include shantytown and transport improvements. The Francistown Project in Botswana succeeded in giving 95% of households clean water, roads, and street lighting. Squatters were given legal tenure.

In the last decade "sites and services" schemes have concentrated on providing water, sanitation, street foundations and power, but left construction of housing to individual occupants. This policy has evolved into "upgrading" of existing slums and shanties. One project in Lusaka, Zambia, in the '70s tackled the upgrading and servicing of 31 000 plots, bringing basic needs to about 30% of people.

F Whenever cityward migrations have reached unusual proportions, conventional housing and infrastructure services have been hard-pressed to cope. The many millions of poor people now crowding into slums and squatter settlements cannot afford even the simplest permanent housing schemes (86% of urban populations in Bangladesh, for instance, are below the absolute poverty line).

Authorities are being forced to take a different line, tackling only the most basic provision themselves, and letting the settlers do the rest, with minimal aid. Just one of their intractable problems is that of water supply which is often privately owned – and very scarce. The most urgent need, however, is for greater rural investment to slow the flood to the cities.

DISCUSSION

Question 1 (Section C)

Closer reading of this section shows the two paragraphs focus more on community involvement and cooperation than on leadership, therefore heading **iii** is better than **v**.

Question 2 (Section D)

This section talks about the informal sector as a source of jobs, so the best heading is still **vii**.

Question 3 (Section E)

Closer reading of this section shows the World Bank is only mentioned as a provider of funds. There is much more information about the provision of infrastructure in cities, so your choice would be **vi**.

Question 4 (Section F)

There is discussion of several aspects of housing and services for migrants to the city, so **i** is a better choice than **iv**, which is only about housing.

Questions 5–9

As you were reading, did you underline the following: Le Corbusier, Niemeyer, El Salvador, informal economy, World Bank, and between 40% and 60%? If you did, it would be fairly easy for you to find the answers to Questions 5–8. Question 9 asks for the author's suggestion or recommendation. This is often found towards the end of a passage. In this case it is in the last sentence.

Question 5 (Section A)

Le Corbusier and Niemeyer appear to be the names of people, as all the answer choices are occupations. Choices A and C are not broad enough for the designers of cities, which seems to be what this section of the passage is about. Therefore the answer is **B**. Of course, it is possible that you know they are architects.

Question 6 (Section C)

The example of El Salvador immediately follows the sentence 'Community involvement and leadership are critical.' It is followed by information between commas which is less important, so the main sentence here reads 'El Salvador...boasted an almost model scheme.' Because of the context the scheme must be one involving a community self-help scheme as described in the paragraph. The answer is **C**.

Question 7 (Section D)

For this question you should look for numbers and possibly also a % sign. You can find numbers and % signs in several sections of the reading. When you quickly read the sentences containing numbers and % signs, you find that Section D mentions the 'informal economy'. The answer is **B**.

Question 8 (Section E)

The World Bank is mentioned in two sections of the Reading: D and E. But only in section E is it followed by an example of a particular scheme receiving funding: Francistown. The answer is **C**.

Question 9 (Section F)

The last sentence of the reading passage reads 'The most urgent need, however, is for greater rural investment to slow the flood to the cities.' This matches answer choice **A** which is 'invest more in rural areas'.

EXERCISE 1

Time target – 5 minutes

Match these headings with the following short readings.

HEADINGS

Cross–Strait Words	Labour–Law Protest	Export Policy Attacked
Helping Hand	Food Aid Short	Risky Remarks
Killings in Paris	Polls Next Year	Church and State
Apec Delegate	No to Tokyo	No Seats, No Support

A Prime Minister Goh Chok Tong won't call general elections until after January 5, when the current parliamentary term ends.

B Taipei will send business tycoon and senior ruling-party official Koo Chen-fu to the November 25–26 summit meeting of the Asia–Pacific Economic Cooperation forum in the Philippines.

C A Vatican delegation to Hanoi helped re-start dialogue that had been stalled for 18 months over Hanoi's refusal to accept the Church's choices of senior church leaders in Vietnam.

D In a rare exchange with a senior Chinese official, Chief Planning Minister P. K. Chiang told China's Foreign Minister Qian Qichen that Taiwan had deserved to be represented at the Asia–Pacific Economic Cooperation forum summit meeting by President Lee Teng-hui. Qian replied that Taiwan was "an economy, not a sovereign country." Chiang said that Taiwan should be treated as an equal of Apec's other members.

E Separatist Tamil Tiger rebels blamed Colombo for the killing of two Tamils who were shot in Paris on October 27.

F Seoul rejected Japan's request to halt construction of a pier on a disputed island in the Sea of Japan that South Korea calls Tokdo and Japan calls Takeshima.

G Malaysia's Foreign Minister Abdullah Ahmad Badawi met Prime Minister Gen. Than Shwe in Rangoon on October 21, the Myanmar News Agency said. Kuala Lumpur said it would help Rangoon in its bid for full membership into the Association of Southeast Asian Nations.

H House National Security Committee Chairman Floyd Spence said Washington's export policy towards China jeopardises national security.

I Thousands of workers took to the streets in Seoul on November 24 in reaction to comments by Labour Minister Jin Nyum that Seoul would overhaul controversial laws curbing union power by year-end.

J Washington won't support expanding the United Nations Security Council unless Germany and Japan are given permanent seats, the American deputy ambassador to the UN said.

K Chief Cabinet Secretary Seiroku Kajiyama angered Seoul when he said an emergency on the Korean peninsula could bring "fake refugees" to Japan and cause street fighting between rival factions of Korean residents. Kajiyama apologised after the South Korean Foreign Ministry expressed "shock" at "remarks that were not friendly to national reunification of the Korean peninsula."

L The government resumed food shipments to Tamil refugees displaced by heavy fighting in the north, ending a three-week blockade.

You can check your answers in the Answer Key.

EXERCISE 2

For this exercise, match the headings with the sections of the text. Remember to do this first of all by reading only the first sentence of each paragraph. Only read the remainder of the text to confirm your first choices.

Time target – 10 minutes

HEADINGS

(i)	Displaced workers
(ii)	Temperate fruit exports
(iii)	Poor health facilities
(iv)	North–South migration
(v)	Chile's exports
(vi)	Jobs are not permanent
(vii)	Low pay for workers, high profits for growers
(viii)	Chile's fruit exports
(ix)	Fruit industry jobs
(x)	Pesticides for the fruit industry

READING PASSAGE

A Under Pinochet, Chilean fruit exports boomed. The country has remained a major supplier of temperate fruits – grapes, nectarines, plums, peaches, pears and apples – to North America and Europe. More than 95 per cent of grape imports to the US are from Chile. Highly perishable exports prompted Cardoen Industries, better known for its weapons and explosives, to produce refrigerated containers for sea and air shipments. Almost all Chile's orchards are less than one hundred miles from a seaport. Over half of Chile's fruit exports are controlled by five transnational companies.

B Most of the estimated half a million jobs created by the fruit industry are temporary and seasonal. Over two-thirds of the labour force in Chile is now employed on a temporary basis, 60 per cent of whom work in the fruit sector.

C In the late 1980s in a major fruit-growing valley, temporary workers, employed for about three months of the year, were paid between $2 and $4 per day; one hectare (2.5 acres) of grapes in the valley earned the owner just under $5000.

D Many of these workers used to be smallholders or agricultural workers who were evicted from plots in Chile's central valley region to make way for commercial producers. Many temporary fruit workers migrate from north to south each year, following the peak moments in the harvest.

E Workers complain of crowded, squalid barracks and limited washing and sanitary facilities, critical for those regularly exposed to pesticides. Imports of pesticides increased more than eight-fold between 1976 and 1986. Some 80 per cent of workers in the fruit industry say the problem of health was either "very serious" or "serious".

You can check your answers in the Answer Key.

EXERCISE 3

This next exercise is slightly different, but you should still use the same strategy.

- Read the questions and answer choices on pages 29 and 30.
- Read only the first sentence of each paragraph.
- Make your first answer choice and note it beside the section of the text.
- Read the remainder of the text to finalise your choice.
- Check your answers in the Answer Key.

Time target – 10 minutes

READING PASSAGE

(i) More and more women are now joining the paid labour force worldwide. They represent the majority of the workforce in all the sectors which are expanding as a result of globalisation and trade liberalisation – the informal sector, including subcontracting; export processing or free trade zones; homeworking; and the "flexible", part-time, temporary, low-paid labour force. Even in countries which have low levels of women paid workers, such as the Arab countries, employment is rising.

In South-East Asia, women represent up to 80 per cent of the workforce in the export processing zones, working mainly in the labour-intensive textile, toy, shoe and electronic sectors. In Latin America and the Caribbean, 70 per cent of economically active women are employed in services. Many women in South-East Asia are moving from manufacturing into services.

(ii) Long excluded from many paid jobs and thus economically dependent on husbands or fathers, paid employment has undoubtedly brought economic and social gains to many women. For many previously inexperienced young women, the opportunity to gain financial independence, albeit limited and possibly temporary, has helped break down some of the taboos of their societies and prescriptions on women's behaviour.

Any gains, however, should be seen in a wider context. Declining economic and social conditions throughout the world, in particular declining household incomes, have compelled many women to take any kind of paid work to meet their basic needs and those of their families. The jobs available to them are, in the main, insecure and low-paid with irregular hours, high levels of intensity, little protection from health and safety hazards and few opportunities for promotion.

(iii) Women's high participation in informal employment is partly due to the fact that many jobs in the formal economy are not open to them: they are actively excluded from certain kinds of work or lack access to education and training or have domestic commitments. The increase of women's participation in the informal sector has been most marked in the countries of Sub-Saharan Africa where sharp economic decline and structural adjustment policies have reduced the official job market drastically.

(iv) Job gains for some women have meant losses for others. Female employment in export production is increasing in Bangladesh, Vietnam and El Salvador, for instance, while women in South Korea, Taiwan and Hong Kong are faced with redundancies as the industries which have relied on their labour for three decades (textile, clothing, shoe and electronics) relocate elsewhere. (In South Korea, industries which tend to employ men – steel, petrochemicals, electricity, automobiles, shipbuilding, machinery – have received government subsidies to stay put.)

As domestic markets are opened up to international competition and quotas which restricted the quantity of imports from any one country are abandoned, cheap, subsidised foreign imports are threatening the livelihoods of many women, small producers and entrepreneurs in "cottage industries". In countries such as India and Bangladesh, for instance, more than 90 per cent of economically-active women work in the informal sector at jobs such as hand loom weaving.

(v) Far from escaping patriarchal control, the industrial setting invariably replicates it, the head of the factory taking the place of husband or father. To attract investors, some Asian countries such as Malaysia and Thailand emphasise the "dexterity of the small hands of the Oriental women and traditional attitude of submission". Women workers are particularly exposed to sexual harassment, a form of violence which reflects the subordination they have to submit to to be allowed to work. Complaints often lead to dismissal.

(vi) In general, women are paid less than men are, and women's jobs pay less than men's jobs. On average, most women earn 50 to 80 per cent of men's pay, but there are considerable variations. In Tanzania, which ranks first in the world for pay equality, women earn 92 per cent of what men earn; in Bangladesh, they earn 42 per cent. Women also have less job security and fewer opportunities for promotion. Higher status jobs, even in industries which employ mostly women, tend to be filled by men.

(vii) In addition, women usually have to continue their unpaid domestic and caring work, such as of children, the sick and the elderly, which is often regarded as women's "natural" and exclusive responsibility. Even when they have full-time jobs outside the home, women take care of most household tasks, particularly the preparation of meals, cleaning and childcare. When women become mothers, they often have no option other than to work part-time or accept home work.

Questions 1–7

The reading passage has 7 sections (i–vii).

*Choose the most suitable phrases **A–D** to complete the sentences below.*

> *Example*   *Answer*
>
> The best title for this text is
>
> **A**   Women in Development
>
> **B**   A Woman's Work is Never Done   **B**
>
> **C**   A Woman's Place is in the Home
>
> **D**   Women as Temporary Workers

1   The reading passage is mainly about

     A   the social position of women

     B   the situation of the working mother

     C   the situation of women in the developing world

     D   the situation of women as paid workers

2   Section **(i)** is mainly about

     A   the paid labour force

     B   women working part-time

     C   more women in the labour force

     D   lack of female workers in Arab countries

3   Section **(ii)** is mainly about

     A   how women benefit and lose from work opportunities

     B   breaking down social taboos

     C   young women gaining experience from work

     D   women working to fulfil basic needs

4   Section **(iv)** is mainly about

     A   women being threatened

     B   the effects of competition and quotas on women's incomes

     C   women becoming redundant as industries relocate

     D   how women have been disadvantaged in the job market

5 Section **(v)** highlights the point that

    A Oriental women have small hands

    B men are still in positions of authority over women

    C women usually work for their husband or their father

    D women who complain are dismissed

6 Section **(vi)** emphasises the point that

    A there are variations in the amount women are paid

    B men generally get the top jobs

    C men get better treatment than women do

    D women in Bangladesh earn less than women in Tanzania do

7 Section **(vii)** is mainly about

    A the extent of women's work

    B women's natural role

    C why women work part-time

    D women doing menial tasks

Specific Information Questions

These questions focus mainly on factual information and relationships between facts in a reading. They can take many forms, such as:
- multiple-choice questions
- questions requiring a short answer
- completing sentences
- matching lists of items
- classifying lists of items
- deciding whether or not the information in the question matches the information in the text.

The strategy you should use for answering these questions is:
- check the instructions quickly
- read the questions
- read any answer choices and predict possible answers
- read the text very quickly, looking for words, phrases or numbers from the questions and answer choices. Also look for synonyms to words in the answer choices
- mark these words, numbers or phrases in the reading.

Time target – 15 minutes

This practice uses Reading 2 from Practice Reading test 1. It gives you further practice choosing headings to match sections of the reading. See if you can do it more efficiently than you did it the first time. It also gives you practice with questions where you have to decide if the information in the question is the same as the information in the reading. Use the appropriate strategies for each question type.

Step 1 – Match the headings
- Read the headings.
- Read the first sentence of each paragraph.
- Tentatively assign one or two headings to each section.

Step 2 – Answer the remaining questions and confirm your choice of headings
- Read the remaining questions and guess a possible answer. (Even though you may not be able to guess the answer, trying to will help you think about the question.)
- Read the passage quickly.
- Mark possible answers.
- Decide the most appropriate headings.
- Quickly go back to sections you marked and answer the remaining questions.
- Write your answers on your answer sheet in the correct boxes.

READING PASSAGE 2

You should spend about 20 minutes on Questions 14–25 which are based on Reading Passage 2.

Reading Passage 2 has 6 sections A–F.

Questions 14–18

From the following list of headings choose the most suitable heading for Sections A–F.

Write the appropriate numbers (i–ix) in boxes 14–18 on your answer sheet.

Note: *There are more headings than sections so you will not use all of*
them. You may use any of the headings more than once.

HEADINGS

(i)	Increasing popularity of pets in Australia
(ii)	Dogs in cities
(iii)	Benefits of pet ownership
(iv)	Pet ownership in Australia
(v)	Private open space and landscaping
(vi)	Criticisms of pet ownership in Australian cities
(vii)	Keeping pets under control
(viii)	Pet owners' obligations
(ix)	Housing and precinct design
(x)	Pet research

Example	*Answer*
Section E	**ix**

14   Section A

15   Section B

16   Section C

17   Section D

18   Section F

DOMESTIC PETS IN NEW URBAN AREAS

The role of urban design in successful pet ownership

This paper summarises the findings of an investigation into the role of urban design in successful pet ownership. There are several reasons why planners should consider pets in decisions about residential and open space development.

A   People are not generally aware of the popularity of pet ownership in Australia. The Morgan Research surveys estimate that in 1992, 37% of Australian households owned one or more dogs, and 30% owned one or more cats. Fifty-three per cent of all households owned either a dog or a cat. Pet-owning households are clearly a substantial group within the community.

B   Research shows that pets play an important role in teaching children about sharing, caring, communication and responsibility. They also act as companions and protectors, stress relievers and in some cases help to foster family cohesion. While pets are traditionally associated with family-type households, they are just as important to households without children – indeed they are often surrogates for children in childless families. This applies particularly to the elderly, who usually form very close associations with their pets. In an era when the population is ageing and more people are living alone, pets can provide valuable relief from loneliness.

C   Urban pet management has been the subject of extensive debate among veterinarians and those involved in local government for some time. Part of the reason is that people complain more readily about other people's pets than ever before. Emphasis on urban consolidation has meant that smaller homes and back gardens and multi-dwelling developments not only discourage people from owning pets but also place greater demands on scarce public open space. Pet owners may face tougher restrictions from either their local council or resident management committee.

D   The term socially responsible pet ownership has emerged to describe a set of responsibilities to which pet owners are now expected to adhere. In meeting their responsibilities pet owners need to consider:

- Providing an enriching environment to reduce unwanted behaviour; e.g. excessive barking.

- Confining dogs to their premises. The advantages of this include protection from catching disease, being run over and fighting. Ideally cats should be confined to the house at night for their own protection where practicable.

- Training pets to alter unacceptable behaviour.

- Exercising dogs, especially if they spend long periods on their own.

E It might be tempting to prescribe different pets for different types of housing. Some people already have firm views about pets and housing type, mostly in relation to dogs, e.g. that the only environment for a dog is in conventional detached housing or that a "big" dog is only suitable in the country. However, suitability is as much dependent on the quality of space as it is on the quantity.

A dwelling that overlooks areas of activity is ideal for pets because it increases the amount of stimulation that can be received from the property, e.g. dwellings that overlook a park or are adjacent to a busy street. This is one way to alleviate boredom and the negative behaviours that sometimes result.

Preferably a dog should have access to some outdoor space. Open space is not essential for a cat provided an enriching environment is maintained indoors, e.g. a bay window or internal fernery. Ideally dogs should have access to all areas of open space on a property. On the whole a dog's behaviour is likely to be better if he or she can see the street. Although the dog may bark at passers-by in the street, there will be less likelihood of excessive barking that might arise through boredom. Providing a dog with surveillance of the street also enhances public security — a very positive benefit.

F With adequate fencing, a dog will be confined to the property. Cats are less easily constrained and are discussed below. The standard paling fence will restrain almost all dogs. They are recommended for side and rear boundaries. Solid front fences limit the view of the outside world and are not recommended. The dog will tend to be less roused by sound stimuli if he or she can see passers-by or activities in the street. However, it is important to ensure that the dog cannot get through the fence. Furthermore, all gates should be fitted with a return spring self-closing device.

Cats are not as easily restrained as dogs as they are more agile and have quite different notions of territoriality. Mostly this does not create a problem, although difficulties may arise in environmentally sensitive areas where cats may prey on wildlife. It is recommended that cats be confined to the house at night for their own protection.

The pleasures and benefits of pet ownership should be available to everyone. However, owning a pet brings with it responsibilities to which we are increasingly being called to adhere. It is hoped that the guidelines will encourage people to think about pets in decisions about residential and community development. If they do, pet ownership will not be prejudiced by the push for urban consolidation.

Questions 19–24

Do the following statements reflect the claims of the writer of Reading Passage 2?

In boxes 19–24 on your answer sheet write:

YES   *if the statement agrees with the writer*

NO   *if the statement contradicts the writer*

NOT GIVEN   *if there is no information about this in the passage*

19   Research shows that more than half of Australian families have both a cat and a dog.

20   Many pets get lonely when their owners are away from home.

21   Although having outdoor space available is good for cats and dogs, it is not absolutely essential.

22   While fences are good for keeping dogs off the streets, they should not block the animal's view of street activities.

23   Dogs should be encouraged to bark at everybody going by.

24   It is safer for cats if they are kept in the house at night.

Question 25

Which of the following statements A–D best reflects the views of the writer of Reading Passage 2?

*Choose the appropriate letter **A–D** and write it in box 25 on your answer sheet.*

A   Although many people keep dogs in the city, this is not truly a suitable environment for them.

B   Although the city is less satisfactory than the country for keeping pets, it is still recommended that families with children and older people have a pet of some kind.

C   Keeping pets in cities is appropriate so long as the owners ensure they do not annoy others.

D   Having a pet in the city can be a rewarding experience for all concerned provided sensible precautions are taken to ensure the pet has a satisfactory environment.

DISCUSSION

Your initial reading of the first sentence of each paragraph should have enabled you to make the following choices.

Heading **(ix)** is the heading for Section E in the example. Therefore, you will probably not use it again.

Section A (Question 14)

The two key words in the headings and the first sentence are 'popularity' and 'ownership'. Therefore, you should note both **(i)** and **(iv)** beside this section.

Section B (Question 15)

The key words and phrases here are 'research' and 'benefits' in the headings with 'play an important role' in the first sentence. So you should note **(iii)** and **(x)** beside this section.

Section C (Question 16)

The key words here are 'criticisms' and 'cities' in the headings. In the first sentence of the passage, there are no exact matches for these, but there are synonyms. The most obvious is 'urban' for cities. 'The subject of extensive debate' is another clue here. If there is public debate over a matter, this generally indicates that some people are criticising the situation. Note **(vi)** beside Section C.

Section D (Question 17)

The phrases 'Pet owners' and 'pet ownership' are almost the same and 'obligations' are similar to responsibility, so 'socially responsible' is relevant here. Put **(viii)** beside Section D.

Section F (Question 18)

The first sentence of paragraph 1 talks about confinement of dogs. So **(ii)** might be appropriate, but the first sentence of paragraph 2 talks about restraining cats. The heading 'Keeping pets under control' is broader than either of these and covers both. So choose **(vii)** for this.

You should not have chosen **(v)** for any of them at this point, though it might apply to either Section E or F. Therefore, you should have kept it in mind when you read the passage more carefully.

Question 19

The information you need to answer this question is in the first paragraph which gives figures on pet ownership in Australia. The relevant sentence says 'Fifty-three per cent of all households owned either a dog or a cat.' The statement for question 19 says '...more than half of Australian families have both a cat and a dog.' The answer is **N** or **NO**.

Question 20

The reading talks about dogs needing exercise if they are alone a lot and also talks about dogs being bored. However, there is no mention of pets being lonely when they are left alone. While you may believe that pets get lonely when they are left alone, there is nothing in this passage about pets being lonely. The answer is **NG** or **NOT GIVEN**.

Question 21

Section E is where you should look for the answer to this question. This section talks about pets having a **quality** environment with plenty of stimulation. The third paragraph in this section says that it is **preferable** for a dog to have outdoor space. It also says 'open space is not essential for a cat'. Therefore you can conclude that outdoor space is good for pets but it is **not absolutely essential** so the answer is **Y** or **YES**.

Question 22

The answer to this question can be found in Section F. The first sentence of this section points out that fences are effective for keeping dogs off the street. The fifth sentence here says 'Solid front fences limit the view of the outside world and are not recommended.' The answer is **Y** or **YES**.

Question 23

The answer to this is in the last paragraph of Section E, which says 'Although the dog may bark at passers-by in the street, there will be less likelihood of excessive barking.' The use of 'excessive' (which means too much) tells you that barking is not desirable. Therefore you can see that dogs should **not** be encouraged to bark. The answer is **N** or **NO**.

Question 24

This sentence is a paraphrase of the last sentence of the second paragraph in Section F. The answer is **Y** or **YES**.

Question 25

This question requires you to decide which answer choice best summarises the views of the writer. The sections on Viewpoint Questions and Summarising Questions will give you more practice with questions like this. In this case you should choose **D** as this most closely reflects the main points of the reading.

A is not suitable because it contradicts what the writer says.

B could be said to partially reflect the views of the writer, but only on one or two points.

C does reflect the views of the writer, but the focus is wrong. This choice focuses on people rather than on pets.

D reflects the views of the writer, and summarises the main points with the focus on pets.

EXERCISE 4

Time target – 10 minutes

In this exercise you can practise two types of specific information questions: short answer questions and multiple-choice questions. In the IELTS test, these questions usually follow the reading. Nevertheless, you should turn to the questions first and:

- read the instructions quickly
- read the questions
- read the answer choices for the multiple-choice questions
- predict possible answers for both types.

In this reading passage you should use the headings and the typographic conventions to help you quickly scan to find the answers. For example, if the question asks about WHO, then you scan the passage to find those capitalised letters.

READING PASSAGE

UNICEF, MALNUTRITION AND MICRONUTRIENTS

UNICEF has continued to be at the forefront of advocacy and support for the implementation of programs to combat child malnutrition. A condition for designing effective programs to fight malnutrition is understanding the causes of the problem and recognising how complex they are.

Micronutrients

IODINE: Some of the most rapid and important progress in UNICEF programs is in the area of salt iodisation. The strategy of universal salt iodisation (USI) has been widely accepted in all regions, and the goal of USI by end-1995 has been met in virtually all of Latin America and in many countries in other regions. During the year, a number of countries with a high prevalence of iodine deficiency in which salt iodisation was previously thought to be virtually impossible, such as Pakistan and Indonesia, started to iodise at least half of all salt reaching consumers. To achieve this, UNICEF offices supported a range of innovative and flexible approaches, for example the establishment of an "Iodised Salt Support Facility" in Pakistan, to provide training, supplies and quality control to the 800 or so small salt crushers in the country.

Enormous progress was seen not only in getting iodine into salt but also in the promulgation of laws to give teeth to monitoring and quality control efforts. UNICEF, WHO and the International Council for the Control of Iodine Deficiency Disorders (ICCIDD) sponsored a forum in 1995 to consider the iodisation and monitoring challenges faced by countries in which salt is brought to market by many small producers rather than larger enterprises.

A technical monograph on practical ways of monitoring salt iodisation programs was developed jointly with WHO, ICCIDD and PAMM and widely distributed. Many UNICEF country programs are monitoring household availability of iodised salt, utilising a simple test kit, as part of the Multi-Indicator Cluster Surveys being undertaken to assess progress in meeting the goals of the World Summit.

VITAMIN A: WHO–UNICEF estimates now indicate that over 250 million children still suffer from vitamin A deficiency (VAD) with many millions more at risk. The known effects of VAD on the immune system and thus on child mortality make this a high-priority challenge for UNICEF. In 1995, UNICEF supported surveys of vitamin A status that resulted in widespread deficiency being recognised for the first time in Egypt, South Africa, Kenya and Botswana.

With support from the Micronutrient Initiative in Canada, UNICEF launched projects in 14 countries that will enable innovation in systems of distribution of vitamin A supplements and improvements in monitoring the mortality and morbidity impact of supplementation. A number of countries are building on the successful experience of Guatemala in fortification of sugar with vitamin A. Bolivia and Brazil both launched sugar fortification with vitamin A on a pilot basis in 1995. In Namibia and South Africa, the feasibility of fortifying maize meal with vitamin A is being considered.

UNICEF supports dietary diversification and the consumption of appropriate fruits and vegetables as one of the most potentially sustainable ways for communities to overcome micronutrient malnutrition. Research completed in 1995 with UNICEF assistance pointed to the need to pay further attention to the types of vegetables grown and the type of cooking in order to maximise the impact of home gardening on the vitamin A status of children. In Bangladesh, UNICEF is collaborating with Helen Keller International to assess the impact of a large home gardening project on the vitamin A status of mothers and young children. This information should help to ensure that future programs of this type are designed in the most cost effective way.

IRON: The statement on strategies for reducing iron deficiency anaemia, developed and adopted by WHO and UNICEF in 1995, calls for general supplementation with iron in any population of pregnant women or young children where the prevalence of anaemia exceeds 30%. The results of research trials investigating the impact on anaemia of weekly iron supplements have started to become available. Weekly iron or iron and vitamin A supplements now appear to be a feasible intervention to combat iron deficiency anaemia on a population basis in some vulnerable groups.

UNICEF supported a meeting, jointly with the Thrasher Research Fund and Cornell University, to explore ways of increasing the micronutrient content of foods commonly consumed in countries where micronutrient malnutrition is common. Plant breeders, soil scientists and human nutritionists met to consider the problem and agreed that the micronutrient content of foods had been neglected in the breeding of high yielding (green revolution) varieties of cereals such as rice. With the realisation of the tremendous importance of the micronutrient content of staple food crops to human development, plant breeders agreed that future breeding work should take micronutrient goals into account. The participants also called for research in other priority areas to exploit the potential food-based systems, including the development of programs and policies that influence the choices of consumers and producers to increase the supply and consumption of micronutrient-rich foods.

Questions 1–4

*Using **NO MORE THAN THREE WORDS**, answer the following questions according to the passage.*

1   What strategy for overcoming iodine deficiency did UNICEF plan to have in place by the end of 1995?

2 & 3   In which two countries was iodised salt thought unlikely to succeed?

4   What did WHO, PAMM and ICCIDD collaborate to produce?

Questions 5–8

*Choose the appropriate letter **A–D** to answer Questions 5–8.*

5 In which country or area was an "Iodised Salt Support Facility" established?

    A Indonesia

    B Latin America

    C Botswana

    D Pakistan

6 What common food has vitamin A been added to?

    A salt

    B maize meal

    C sugar

    D rice flour

7 Why does UNICEF support fruit and vegetable consumption and a more varied diet?

    A it's cheaper

    B it's sustainable

    C it's more easily obtainable

    D it's more cost effective

8 In what aspect of the green revolution was micronutrient content not taken fully into account?

    A development of high-yielding varieties of cereals

    B excessive use of pesticides

    C programs designed to influence consumer choice

    D application of chemical fertilisers

You can check your answers in the Answer Key.

EXERCISE 5

Time target – 15 minutes

Another form that specific information questions might take involves completing information in a diagram or a table. In this exercise you will practise this as well as sentence completion questions. They are similar to short answer questions, which you did in Exercise 4. In the IELTS test, these questions usually follow the reading. Remember you should turn to the questions first and:
- read the instructions quickly
- read the questions
- study the table or diagram
- read the sentence beginnings
- predict possible answers
- check your answers in the key.

READING PASSAGE

TRAINING

Training continues to be a major element of labour market reform in Australia. To provide the information necessary for the analysis of training issues and the development and evaluation of training policies and programs, the Australian Bureau of Statistics (ABS) has conducted a number of training surveys.

Training expenditure

Estimates of the expenditure by employers on the formal training of their employees, and of the paid time employees spent receiving formal training were collected in the 1993 Employer Training Expenditure survey, which covered the September quarter 1993. The survey defined formal training as all training activities which have a structured plan and format designed to develop job related skills and competence, and found that total expenditure on formal training during 1 July to 30 September 1993 by Australian employers was estimated at $1 100 million.

Who received training?

The 1993 Survey of Training and Education found that in the twelve months prior to the survey being undertaken, an estimated 86% of those who had a wage or salary job in the previous twelve months undertook some form of training. The greatest proportion of wage or salary earners by occupation who undertook training in 1993 were professionals. An estimated 96% of professionals received some form of training in the twelve month period and 70% undertook study or training courses. Among blue-collar workers, clerks at 89% received more training than salespersons and personal service workers, though the latter attended slightly more study courses. Plant and machine operators, and drivers had the lowest proportion receiving some form of training (72%), with labourers receiving slightly more.

Length of training course

Of the 5 581 900 wage and salary earners who attended an in-house training course in the twelve months prior to the survey, some 35% of the courses lasted 40 hours or more. Male participants had more attendances at these longer courses than did female participants (42% compared with 27%).

Reasons for training employees

The 1994 Training Practices Survey found that 32% of Australian employers reported providing some formal training for their employees during the twelve month period ending February 1994. Improved work performance was reported by 80% of employers as a reason for training employees. The next two most common reasons for training were to enable employees to move to other positions within the organisation, and to multi-skill employees, (reported by 41% and 40% of employers respectively). Almost half the employers who reported training (44%) also reported that their training expenditure increased during the previous twelve months. Technological change was the factor most often reported as having increased training expenditure (30% of employers), followed by quality assurance (26% of employers). Time constraints and cost constraints were reported as the most common limitations to the amount of training provided by employers for their employees (56% and 41% of employers respectively).

Almost all employers who formally trained employees used external training providers to meet part, or all of their training needs (92%). A lesser proportion (62%) reported providing in-house training for their employees during the reference period. In February 1994, it is estimated that employers in Australia employed 15 800 full-time trainers to provide training for their employees. There was approximately one full-time trainer for every three hundred and fifty employees.

Complete the vertical axis on the table below.

Choose NO MORE THAN THREE WORDS from the passage for each answer.

Training undertaken by wage or salary earners, 1993 (%)

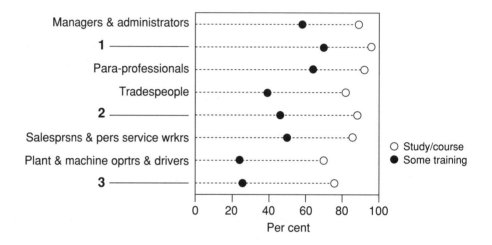

Complete the sentences below with words taken from the Reading passage. Use NO MORE THAN THREE WORDS for each answer.

Having a structured plan is an essential part of ..(4)..

More men than women attended longer in-house ..(5)..

The main reason employers provided training for their employees was to improve their ..(6)..

Two factors leading to higher training costs were ..(7).. and ..(8)..

Most training was provided through the use of ..(9)..

DISCUSSION

Questions 1–3

In this exercise you have to complete the descriptors on the vertical axis of a graph; in this case occupations in a hierarchy based on job levels. For Question 1 the most likely occupation to fit between 'managers and administrators' and 'para-professionals' would be 'professionals'. Questions 2 and 3 are rather more difficult, but the two major groups clearly absent from the axis are general office workers or clerical staff and manual workers. These might be possible answers for 2 and 3 respectively. Remember, you must choose words from the passage for your answers.

Questions 4–9

The grammar helps. Each of these answers requires a noun. Words modifying nouns are other nouns and adjectives, so you might also need another noun or an adjective. You will need to be careful about the type of noun. There are no articles (the, a, an) given and the IELTS does not normally require an article as part of the answer, so this would suggest that the nouns you need will be either plural or abstract nouns. A quick reading of the subheadings in the passage and the questions tells you that the reading is about job training, so for Question 4 one possibility is the word 'training'. However, something more specific is probably needed, so look for an appropriate adjective or another noun to say what kind of training.

The sentence in Question 5 could also be completed with the word 'training', but it is unlikely that two questions in a row will require exactly the same answer.

Question 6: What are employers mainly interested in? Profits. The more employees produce, the better the profits, so probably the employers want to improve the productive capability or the productivity of their employees.

Questions 7 and 8: What could make training cost more? There are quite a few possibilities, so this is quite difficult to predict, but you could watch out for such possibilities as the costs of trainers, facilities, technology, etc. What others can you think of?

Question 9: Who or what can provide training? The answer can be people or institutions, so be alert for these. People could be trainers, instructors, or specialists while institutions could be colleges, universities, companies, etc. What others can you think of?

Were questions 4–9 difficult? There is more practice in using the skills you need for answering questions like these in the section on summary questions (p. 66).

You can check your answers in the Answer Key.

EXERCISE 6

Time target – 5 minutes

This exercise gives you more practice completing information in tables.

READING PASSAGE

SPORT AND RECREATION

A large proportion of Australians, regardless of social position, income and age, participate in some form of sporting activity. The impact of sport extends over a wide range of associated activities in community and commercial fields. Sport is a large industry in Australia encompassing not only participants but also employment within the sporting infrastructure; manufacture of apparel, equipment and other goods (e.g. trophies); tourism and support industries (e.g. printing, media). The sporting activities of Australians include a range of organised and social sport, recreational and leisure activities undertaken both at home and away from home.

Involvement in sport

In March 1993, an ABS survey of persons 15 years of age and over was conducted throughout Australia to obtain information about involvement in sport during the previous 12 months. Involvement in sport was defined to include both paid and unpaid participation in playing and non-playing capacities. Spectator involvement in sport was excluded.

The survey found that one third of the Australian population aged 15 years and over were involved in sport, as players (3.1 million), non-players (0.5 million) or both players and non-players (0.9 million). More men than women were involved as players and as non-players.

Overall, 35% of males played sport compared to 23% of females, and at all ages a greater proportion of males than females played sport. Younger men and women were more likely to play sport than older men and women. Fifty-six per cent of men aged 15 to 24 played sport compared to 39% of women in the same age group. In the 25 to 34 age group 43% of men played sport, compared to 28% of women. Twenty per cent of men and 12% of women aged 65 and over played sport. In Table 11.29 'all players' includes those players who have some non-playing involvement.

Table 11.29	Persons involved in sport, March 1993			
	Males		Females	
Age group (years)	All players	Non-players	All players	Non-players
15–24	55.5	1.3	39.4	1.9
25–34	42.5	3.1	28.1	4.2
35–44	32.3	8.1	20.7	9.1
45–54	25.0	6.8	14.8	4.6
55–64	21.1	3.5	14.5	1.1
65+	20.3	1.1	12.2	0.4
Total	**35.3**	**4.1**	**23.1**	**3.8**

For those involved in sport solely as non-players, the 35 to 44 years age group had the highest participation rate (8% for males, 9% for females). Their most common activities were as administrators or committee members.

Sport and recreation participation

Participation in organised and social sporting activities is measured by a quarterly household survey, the Population Survey Monitor conducted by ABS. This survey showed that in 1993–94 the most popular sport was golf, with 384 600 people participating in organised golf (3% of the population), and a further 128 000 participating in social golf (1% of the population).

The most popular organised sporting activities for men aged 15 and over were golf, outdoor cricket, basketball and Australian rules football. For women aged 15 and over, netball, tennis, aerobics and golf were the most popular organised sporting activities. The most popular sports among those aged 55 and over were golf and lawn bowls.

In addition to organised sports, many people are involved in social sport and other recreational activities. In 1993–94 the most popular social sports were tennis and golf, followed by squash and lawn bowls. In February and May 1995 two of the most popular recreational activities were cycling (614 000 in February, 586 000 in May), and fishing (598 000 in February and 636 000 in May). (See Table 11.31.)

People who do not play sport

When people did not play sport, respondents in the survey were asked why not. The most common reason for not participating in sport, given by 39% of men and 43% of women was injury or illness. Men were more likely than women not to participate in sport because of a sports injury (19% compared to 13%) while women are more likely than men not to participate because of an illness. Twenty-seven per cent of men and 20% of women said they had no time or were too busy to participate in sport. Men were more likely than women to be deterred by bad weather while women were more likely to be prevented from participating in sport because they had no child-care facilities. (See Table 11.32.)

Questions 1–3

Complete the table below.

*Choose **NO MORE THAN THREE WORDS** from the passage for each answer.*

Table 11.31	Persons aged 15 years and over who participated in organised sport, 1993–94 ('000)	
Sport	**Males**	**Females**
..(1)..	..	98.8
Australian rules football	151.4	..
Basketball	153.4	77.7
Cricket (indoor)	91.6	..
Cricket (outdoor)	193.9	..
..(2)..	301.9	80.7
Lawn bowls	115.3	75.2
..(3)..	..	287.1
Soccer (outdoor)	147.2	..
Squash	78.5	46.3
Swimming	..	60.9
Tennis	137.1	162.1

Questions 4–6

Complete the table below.

*Choose **NO MORE THAN THREE WORDS** from the passage for each answer.*

Table 11.32 Main reasons for not participating in sport, persons aged 18 years and over, 1993–94 (%)		
Reasons	**Males**	**Females**
Illness or injury	39.2	43.3
..(4)..	26.7	19.8
..(5)..	7.5	4.1
Transport	1.1	..
..(6)..	0.5	2.6
Expense/cost	0.5	0.9
Other	24.5	29.3
Total	**100.0**	**100.0**

You can check your answers and read the discussion in the Answer Key.

EXERCISE 7

The questions in this exercise focus mainly on classification, although there are other questions to give you more practice. Note that the reading has been divided into two parts. Read the questions and the discussion first.

Time target – 15 minutes for Part I, Questions 1–11

READING PASSAGE – PART I

THEORIES OF JOB SATISFACTION

What makes some people more satisfied with their jobs than others? What underlying processes account for people's feelings of job satisfaction? Insight into these important questions is provided by various theories of job satisfaction. We will describe two of the most influential approaches — Herzberg's *two-factor theory* and Locke's *value theory*.

Herzberg's Two-factor Theory

Think about something that may have happened on your job that made you feel especially satisfied or dissatisfied. What were these events? Over thirty years ago Frederick Herzberg posed this question to more than 200 accountants and engineers, and carefully analysed their responses. What he found was somewhat surprising: different factors accounted for job satisfaction and dissatisfaction.

Although you might expect that certain factors lead to satisfaction when they are present, and dissatisfaction when they are absent, this was *not* the case. Job satisfaction and dissatisfaction were found to stem from different sources. In particular, dissatisfaction was associated with conditions surrounding the jobs (e.g. working conditions, pay, security, quality of supervision, relations with others) rather than the work itself. Because these factors prevent negative reactions, Herzberg referred to them as *hygiene* (or *maintenance*) *factors*. By contrast, satisfaction was associated with factors associated with the work itself or to outcomes directly derived from it, such as the nature of their jobs, achievement in the work, promotion opportunities, and chances for personal growth and recognition. Because such factors were associated with high levels of job satisfaction, Herzberg called them *motivators*. Herzberg's distinction between motivators and hygiene factors is referred to as the **two-factor theory of job satisfaction**.

Research testing Herzberg's theory has yielded mixed results. Some studies have found that job satisfaction and dissatisfaction were based on different factors, and that these are in keeping with the distinction made by Herzberg. Other studies, however, have found that factors labeled as hygienes and motivators exerted strong effects on both satisfaction and dissatisfaction, thereby casting doubt on Herzberg's theory. In view of such equivocal evidence, we must label Herzberg's theory as an intriguing but unverified framework for understanding job satisfaction. Still, the theory is useful for describing the conditions that people find satisfying and dissatisfying on the job. The theory has also been useful in emphasising the importance of factors such as the opportunity for personal growth, recognition, and increased responsibility. Attention to such variables has stimulated much of the research and theory on job enlargement and job enrichment. In this way, Herzberg's theory has contributed much to the field of organisational behaviours, despite the lack of support for some of its key predictions.

Questions 1–6

In Herzberg's 'two-factor theory', which factors would be associated with job satisfaction and job dissatisfaction?

Choose:

S   *for* **Satisfaction**

D   *for* **Dissatisfaction**

1   challenging assignments

2   pension plan

3   achievement

4   holiday and sick leave allowances

5   salary

6   recognition

Questions 7–11

Do the following statements reflect the claims of the writer in the Reading Passage?

Choose:

YES   *if the statement agrees with the writer*

NO   *if the statement contradicts the writer*

NOT GIVEN   *if there is no information about this in the passage*

7   According to Hertzberg, motivators are associated with working conditions while hygiene factors are associated with the work itself.

8   Herzberg's theory is applicable to accountants and engineers but not to other professions.

9   The results from research on Herzberg's theory have been conclusive.

10   Although some research has revealed other factors for job satisfaction and dissatisfaction, the factors are consistent with Herzberg's classification.

11   Herzberg's research enabled him to develop the strategies of job enlargement and job enrichment.

DISCUSSION

Questions 1–6

There is an extra dimension to these questions. This time you need to extend the specific information given in the reading to include other specific information of the same type.

Questions 7–11

These are also more difficult as the statements involve re-wording or para-phrases of the information in the passage. This means you need to look for synonyms. You will have more practice with this strategy in the sections on Viewpoint Questions and Summary Questions.

Another difficulty here is that some of the statements contain information that is not given in the passage. In these cases you have to be very careful not to reach conclusions which are not justified by the information in the passage.

Check your answers and read the discussion in the Answer Key before going on to Part II.

READING PASSAGE – PART II

Locke's Value Theory

A second important theory of job satisfaction is Locke's **value theory**. This conceptualisation claims that job satisfaction exists to the extent that the job outcomes (such as rewards) an individual receives match those outcomes that are desired. The more people receive outcomes they value, the more satisfied they will be; the less they receive outcomes they value, the less satisfied they will be. Locke's approach focuses on *any* outcomes that people value, regardless of what they are, and not necessarily basic lower-order needs. The key to satisfaction in Locke's theory is the *discrepancy* between those aspects of the job one has and those one wants; the greater the discrepancy, the less the satisfaction.

McFarlin and Rice conducted a study that provides good support for value theory. Using a questionnaire, these investigators measured how much of various job facets – such as freedom to work one's own way, learning opportunities, promotion opportunities, and pay level – a diverse group of workers wanted, and how much they felt they already had. They also measured how satisfied the respondents were with each of these facets and how important each facet was to them. As shown in Figure 5.7, an interesting trend emerged: those aspects of the job about which respondents experienced the greatest discrep-ancies were the ones with which they were most dissatisfied, and those with which they experienced the smallest discrepancies were the ones with which they were most satisfied. Interestingly, McFarlin and Rice also found that this relationship was greater among individuals who placed a high amount of satisfaction on a particular facet of the job. In other words, the more important a particular facet of the job was believed to be, the less satisfied people were when they failed to get as much of this facet as they wanted.

An interesting implication of value theory is that it calls attention to the aspects of the job that need to be changed for job satisfaction to result. Specifically, the theory suggests that these aspects might not be the same ones for all people, but any valued aspects of the job about which people perceive serious discrepancies. By emphasising values, Locke's theory suggests that job satisfaction may be derived from many factors. In this respect, it is fully consistent with the findings of research on the causes of job satisfaction.

Questions 12–14

Questions 12 and 13

*Label the lines on the graph. Write the correct letter **A** or **B** for Questions 12 and 13.*

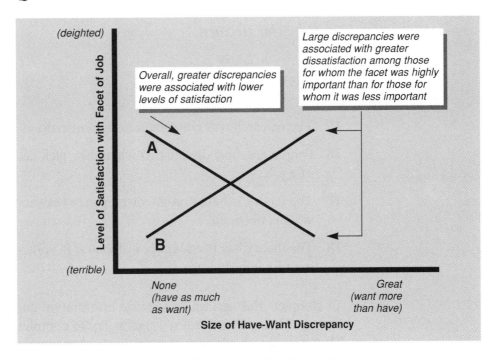

Figure 5.7   Job satisfaction: a result of the discrepancy between what we want and what we have

12 Low importance

13 High importance

Question 14

14 Which of the following best summarises Locke's value theory?

    A The more people get from management, the more they want.

    B People will be satisfied with their work when they get everything the way they want it.

    C In most jobs, it is almost impossible for the conditions leading to job satisfaction to be fulfilled.

    D It is not essential for every aspect of a job to be perfect for a person to feel satisfied with the job.

Questions 15–18

From Parts I and II of the reading, say which of the following apply to the people mentioned in the Reading Passage.

Choose:

    H   *for* **H**erzberg

    L   *for* **L**ocke

    MR   *for* **M**cFarlin and **R**ice

15 The research was conducted using a questionnaire.

16 People are most dissatisfied when they lack access to valued aspects of a job.

17 The theory is based on the discrepancy between what is desired and what is obtained.

18 The theory has been highly influential in spite of the lack of supporting research findings.

To complete this section on specific information questions, do Reading Passage 1 from Practice test 1 again. Try to complete it in 15 minutes. Then you can check your answers in the Answer Key.

Viewpoint questions are always more difficult to answer because you must understand the views and opinions expressed in the reading. The practice with viewpoint questions uses one of the readings you did earlier. Again, the best strategy is to read the questions first and look for the information to answer them as you read the passage. Watch particularly for synonyms and restatements of the questions.

The paragraphs have been numbered for ease of reference in the discussion that follows. To get the best practice, you should answer the questions before you read the discussion.

Practice

Time target – 15 minutes

READING PASSAGE

A WOMAN'S WORK IS NEVER DONE

1 More and more women are now joining the paid labour force worldwide. They represent the majority of the workforce in all the sectors which are expanding as a result of globalisation and trade liberalisation – the informal sector, including subcontracting; export processing or free trade zones; homeworking; and the "flexible", part-time, temporary, low-paid labour force. Even in countries which have low levels of women paid workers, such as the Arab countries, employment is rising.

2 In South-East Asia, women represent up to 80 per cent of the workforce in the export processing zones, working mainly in the labour-intensive textile, toy, shoe and electronic sectors. In Latin America and the Caribbean, 70 per cent of economically active women are employed in services. Many women in South-East Asia are moving from manufacturing into services.

3 Long excluded from many paid jobs and thus economically dependent on husbands or fathers, paid employment has undoubtedly brought economic and social gains to many women. For many previously inexperienced young women, the opportunity to gain financial independence, albeit limited and possibly temporary, has helped break down some of the taboos of their societies and prescriptions on women's behaviour.

4 Any gains, however, should be seen in a wider context. Declining economic and social conditions throughout the world, in particular declining household incomes, have compelled many women to take any kind of paid work to meet their basic needs and those of their families. The jobs available to them are, in the main, insecure and low-paid with irregular hours, high levels of intensity, little protection from health and safety hazards and few opportunities for promotion.

5 Women's high participation in informal employment is partly due to the fact that many jobs in the formal economy are not open to them: they are actively excluded from certain kinds of work or lack access to education and training or have domestic commitments. The increase of women's participation in the informal sector has been most marked in the countries of Sub-Saharan Africa where sharp economic decline and structural adjustment policies have reduced the official job market drastically.

6 Job gains for some women have meant losses for others. Female employment in export production is increasing in Bangladesh, Vietnam and El Salvador, for instance, while women in South Korea, Taiwan and Hong Kong are faced with redundancies as the industries which have relied on their labour for three decades (textile, clothing, shoe and electronics) relocate elsewhere. (In South Korea, industries which tend to employ men – steel, petrochemicals, electricity, automobiles, shipbuilding, machinery – have received government subsidies to stay put.)

7 As domestic markets are opened up to international competition and quotas which restricted the quantity of imports from any one country are abandoned, cheap, subsidised foreign imports are threatening the livelihoods of many women small producers and entrepreneurs in "cottage industries". In countries such as India and Bangladesh, for instance, more than 90 per cent of economically-active women work in the informal sector at jobs such as hand loom weaving.

8 Far from escaping patriarchal control, the industrial setting invariably replicates it, the head of the factory taking the place of husband or father. To attract investors, some Asian countries such as Malaysia and Thailand emphasise the "dexterity of the small hands of the Oriental women and traditional attitude of submission". Women workers are particularly exposed to sexual harassment, a form of violence which reflects the subordination they have to submit to to be allowed to work. Complaints often lead to dismissal.

9 In general, women are paid less than men are, and women's jobs pay less than men's jobs. On average, most women earn 50 to 80 per cent of men's pay, but there are considerable variations. In Tanzania, which ranks first in the world for pay equality, women earn 92 per cent of what men earn; in Bangladesh, they earn 42 per cent. Women also have less job security and fewer opportunities for promotion. Higher status jobs, even in industries which employ mostly women, tend to be filled by men.

10 In addition, women usually have to continue their unpaid domestic and caring work, such as of children, the sick and the elderly, which is often regarded as women's "natural" and exclusive responsibility. Even when they have full-time jobs outside the home, women take care of most household tasks, particularly the preparation of meals, cleaning and child care. When women become mothers, they often have no option other than to work part-time or accept home work

Questions 1–10

Do the following statements reflect the views of the writer in the Reading passage?

Choose:

> **YES**   *if the statement agrees with the writer*
>
> **NO**   *if the statement contradicts the writer*
>
> **NOT GIVEN**   *if there is no information about this in the passage*

1 Women are commonly employed in labour-intensive and service industries.

2 Unemployed men generally encourage their wives to work.

3 Working women have been freed from social taboos.

4 Women have gained more from entering the workforce than they have lost.

5 Women are often forced by circumstances to accept whatever employment they can get.

6 The opening up of domestic markets has greatly benefited cottage industries.

7 The position of women in the workplace generally reflects their position in the wider society.

8 Although their work opportunities have increased, women are generally disadvantaged in the job market.

9 Men are invariably preferred to women when it comes to promotion.

10 Working mothers are generally able to provide their children with a better education.

DISCUSSION

Although this reading includes factual information, it is primarily a passage expressing the views of the writer. You might compare it with the passage 'Theories of Job Satisfaction' (p. 49) which impartially sets out some theories on that topic. You might also compare it with the next reading which is on the same topic (women and work) but which has a different focus.

1 YES   This question is simply a summary of Paragraph 2. The information is basically factual and does not involve viewpoint.

2 NG   There is no information given in the passage about unemployed men.

3 NO   The question statement is too broad. It means that **all** working women have been freed from **all** social taboos. In Paragraph 3, the writer claims that for **many** working women **some** of the taboos have been broken down.

4 NO   The statement contradicts the claim of the writer. Paragraph 3 describes the gains for women. The rest of the passage describes the losses. So although the writer considers there have been some gains, in general he or she sees the losses as greater.

5 YES   This clearly restates the claim in Paragraph 4 that 'Declining economic and social conditions… have compelled many women to take any kind of paid work'. There are four synonyms to words in the question statement here: 'Declining economic and social conditions' are summed up in the general word 'circumstances'; 'have compelled' is synonymous with 'are forced'; 'any kind' is similar to 'whatever' and 'paid work' is synonymous with 'employment'

6 NO   This states exactly the opposite to Paragraph 7 which says 'As domestic markets are opened up… imports are threatening the livelihoods of many women small producers and entrepreneurs in 'cottage industries'.'

7 YES   This is a rephrasing of the first sentence of Paragraph 8. 'Reflect' is a synonym of 'replicate'.

8 YES   The first part of this sentence summarises the information in the first three paragraphs, while the second part summarises the information in Paragraph 9.

9 NO   The last two sentences in Paragraph 9 state that 'Women… have **fewer** opportunities for promotion.' and that 'Higher status jobs… **tend** to be filled by men.' The sentence of the question uses the word 'invariably' which means **always**. Therefore this statement contradicts the writer.

10 NG   Education for children is not discussed anywhere in the passage.

EXERCISE 8

This reading is longer than those you have done so far. It is the maximum length you are likely to get in an IELTS test. It is also more difficult. This length and level of difficulty could occur in the third reading of an IELTS.

The paragraphs have been numbered to make it easier for you to follow the discussion in the Answer Key.

Time target – 20 minutes

READING PASSAGE

UTILISING WOMEN'S SKILLS

Women Working

1 Britain has a higher proportion of economically active women than any of our EC partners, with the exception of Denmark, and the trend towards greater female participation in paid employment seems to be irreversible. The Central Statistical Office's Social Trends report, published at the beginning of this year, forecasts that the number of women in the labour force is likely to increase by 700 000 over the 1990s and that by the end of the decade no less than 45 per cent of workers will be female. It may be questioned whether industry fully utilises them.

2 At present a high proportion of employed women, four out of ten, work part-time compared with only ten per cent of men in employment. This development is in response to the increased opportunities available to realise two distinct goals:

(1) The industrial goal of achieving greater flexibility in working time and working schedules in order to improve the relationship between labour costs and business needs; and

(2) The personal goal of many women of participating responsibly in both economic and domestic-familial activity without subjecting themselves to intolerable strains.

Industry needs part-time workers and women often find part-time work more feasible than full-time.

3 While many more women would doubtless prefer to have full-time employment, most men below early retirement age would see this as a necessity. The traditional images of the "male breadwinner" and the "female housewife and mother" may be breaking down among females but this process is occurring more slowly among males. Men do adopt the role of "househusband", but their number is still small enough to make the examples newsworthy.

4 For this reason, a good deal of female employment, and especially that part of it which involves women with young children, occurs without much corresponding adjustment or accommodation by men or by the institutions which men have created. Men remain "free" to take on their traditional full-time breadwinner roles, but women depend on there being opportunities for them to participate in economic activity at the times and in the locations which fit in with their domestic responsibilities. However "useful" they might be to industry because they do not want the full-time engagements that are not available, their involvement remains unintegrated.

The Waste of Talent

5 In consequence, the talents which exist within this section of the workforce are under-utilised. They serve as "hands" hired usually to perform routine jobs which can be parcelled out in appropriate part-time lots. They may do these extremely satisfactorily and at low overall cost to the employer, but skills and competencies developed in the course of their other experiences including running a household, organising efficient routines, counselling and developing children, etc. may never be given any chance to surface.

6 In addition they have little opportunity to contribute ideas or suggestions around or outside the immediate confines of their particular job. This is because they are not sufficiently woven into the fabric of the organisation to permit their insinuation into discussions at the right moment or with sufficient persistence to ensure that they get a hearing. They are treated as part of a peripheral workforce and their ideas have little chance of entering the mainstream of thought.

7 Against this background there is little chance that they will be either rotated or promoted to any position of responsibility. Research published recently by the Institute of Manpower Studies confirms that women are generally still very underrepresented in management. It found, as many other studies of women at work have done, that although 40 per cent of the current workforce is female, women constitute only 22 per cent of managers and only 2 per cent of senior executives. This also implies that even full-time women and those who do seek to develop a conventional career have little chance of success.

8 This may reflect stereotypical attitudes similar to those which attach to "part-timers": even full-time female employees appear to present a greater risk than full-time men of failing to make the grade as steady, reliable workers. They may declare themselves to be interested in a career, but they are much more likely than a man to succumb to the alternative career of raising children and running a family home. Therefore, so the stereotypical argument runs, they are less worthy of the employer investing training and development resources in them. If a woman is to get on, she has to surmount hurdles without much assistance and support from the employer.

Effective Utilisation

9 In order to utilise female talents at all effectively, it may well be necessary, as many have already argued, to provide some simple logistical supports in the form of flexible work schedules, child-care facilities and the like. But it may be even more necessary to provide greater opportunity for working women in general and part-time workers in particular, to become integrated into the mainstream of organised activity.

10 This can occur only if industry then treats them as worthy of it, no matter whether they are "merely" part-time or whether they choose to take some time out to start a family. Some organisations, especially those facing a tight labour market, do provide such opportunities and do attempt to keep those on leave of absence in touch with policies and practices. They are probably too few for comfort and too often stimulated by extremely short-sighted and short-lived motives. Unless these activities are integrated with the business strategy, they are unlikely to survive a slackening of the labour market or to give industry full benefit.

11 Finally, their potential is unlikely to be realised unless they are included in all the communication systems developed both to inform employees and to elicit their suggestions for improvement. Part-timers particularly, but also those who perform what have traditionally been regarded as women's jobs, are often excluded from these, so that their often unblinkered views are ignored.

Questions 1–11

Do the following statements reflect the views of the writer in the Reading passage.

Choose:

YES   *if the statement agrees with the writer*

NO   *if the statement contradicts the writer*

NOT GIVEN   *if there is no information about this in the passage*

1   Denmark is the only EC country with fewer economically active women than Britain.

2   The coincidence of women's personal choices and industry's business needs has resulted in large numbers of women working part-time.

3   Women may prefer to be employed full-time; however, men consider it essential.

4   Too many women are taking jobs that rightfully belong to men.

5   Men accept changing perceptions of traditional gender roles more slowly than women do.

6   Skills involved in running a household are unlikely to be of much use in industry.

7   Since women are rarely fully integrated into an organisation, they are unable to contribute useful ideas.

8   One reason women's views are not considered is because they do not understand business strategy.

9   Recent research shows more and more women are moving into management positions.

10   Most full-time female employees are not really interested in a career, even though they may claim to want one.

11   Most of the organisations which have instituted integrative practices have done so only because there has been a shortage of labour.

Question 12

Which sentence best summarises the views of the writer?

Choose the appropriate letter A–D for your answer.

A It is more appropriate for women to work part-time in order that their skills can be fully utilised in homemaking.

B Industry would be far more likely to promote women if they did not take time away from work for their family duties.

C Women have developed a wide range of skills in the home and those skills should be utilised more effectively in industry.

D Although industry has been keen to utilise women's skills, it has been hampered by the lack of government support programs.

EXERCISE 9

Time target – 20 minutes

READING PASSAGE

THE CHANGING NATURE OF CAREERS

As time marches on, the nature of people's jobs changes and the characteristics of organisations change — and as a result, so too do people's careers. According to Schein, these changes can be characterised as developments along three basic dimensions summarised in his *career cone* (see Figure 6.10). First, careers often involve *vertical movement* – that is, promotions up an organisational hierarchy (such as from assistant manager to manager). Naturally, different people working in different settings experience vertical movement at tremendously different rates. Not only may people be prepared for advancement at different times, but also organisations may have different opportunities for promotion. In today's organisations, in which layers of management are being reduced all the time, there are fewer rungs in the organisational ladder, making opportunities for vertical movement more limited than they used to be.

Second, careers often involve *horizontal movement*. This reflects changes in specific job functions, or sometimes, in major fields or specialties. For example, individuals who start out in marketing may move into the related field of sales. In recent years, growing numbers of people have been willing to make such horizontal moves, even though doing so may involve a considerable amount of retraining. This trend may result from several sources, such as people's needs to seek fulfilment by doing different kinds of work, or by their belief that they might sooner be able to make a vertical movement by first moving horizontally into a field with greater opportunities for advancement.

Finally, careers also involve what Schein terms *radial movement* — shifts toward or away from the inner circle of management in an organisation, the base of power. Such movement often follows vertical movement (i.e. promotion), but not always. For example, a manager of engineering operations for a television network, who works at its headquarters, may be promoted to the vice president at one of the network's local affiliates. The promotion in this case is real, but the individual is now farther away from the organisation's inner circle of power than before (both literally in terms of miles and figuratively in terms of influence).

At the same time careers develop along these three dimensions, they also seem to move through repeated cycles of stability and change. Soon after an individual has been hired or promoted into a new position, a stage of *career growth* occurs. During this period, individuals consolidate their recent gains by acquiring the new skills and information needed to perform their current jobs effectively. As this process is completed, they enter a stage of *stabilisation*, in which they are performing their jobs to their fullest capacity and things are on an even keel (for the time being, at least). This is followed by a period of *transition* in which individuals prepare themselves psychologically for their next move upward. During this period, they anticipate the demands of their next stage and get ready to meet them. When the expected promotion arrives, the cycle starts over again. In short, the careers of many individuals are marked by a process in which they grow into each new position, become acclimatised to it, and then begin preparations for the next step on the ladder.

Questions 1–3

Label Schein's career cone to show the three basic types of movement involved in career change.

*Choose **ONE OR TWO WORDS** from the passage for your answers.*

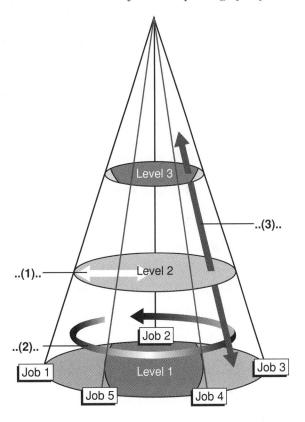

Figure 6.10

Questions 4–12

Do the following statements reflect the claims of the writer of the Reading passage.

Choose:

> **YES** *if the statement agrees with the writer*
>
> **NO** *if the statement contradicts the writer*
>
> **NOT GIVEN** *if there is no information about this in the passage*

4 There are not so many opportunities for promotion as there once were.

5 The main reason people make horizontal career moves is because they are unhappy with their present work.

6 More people are changing careers because promotional opportunities are limited.

7 Promotions involving radial movement are not really promotions.

8 Once a person has moved away from the centre of power they are unlikely to get back to it.

9 People generally prefer a vertical career change to a horizontal one.

10 The transitional stage of career growth occurs after the person is able to perform their present job effectively.

11 It is not possible for one person to experience all three types of career movement.

12 The career cone illustrates the stages of career growth.

Questions 13–19

Classify the following career changes as associated with:

V Vertical movement

H Horizontal movement

R Radial movement

13 accountant to financial director

14 librarian to publishing editor

15 head office manager to overseas affiliate director

16 accounts director to branch manager

17 class teacher to head teacher

18 factory worker to foreman

19 nurse to hospital registrar

Summarising Questions

Summarising questions can be in the form of:
- a brief summary of part of the reading passage
- a brief summary of the whole reading passage
- notes on the reading passage.

They are usually the last questions related to a reading.

The information in the summary usually has the same sequence as the information in the reading.

They require you to complete gaps in the summary with appropriate words:
- from a box of possible answers
- from the reading passage itself.

The words you have to use are never articles (a, an, the) or prepositions (e.g. at, in, over). They are always what we call content words. They are nouns, verbs, adjectives or adverbs. For this reason a good knowledge of grammar and vocabulary can help you a lot in answering these questions.

As these are usually the last questions for a reading passage, the best strategy for these questions is:

- to read the summary
- if there are words given in a box, to guess an answer
- if you have to find words in the passage, to guess a probable answer
- if you can't immediately guess an answer, to think about the kind of word you need.

The practice and the exercises for summary questions are all based on passages you have already read in working through this book. This is because summary questions usually come last in a set of questions attached to a reading passage, so you will already be familiar with the content of the reading before you try to do these questions.

Practice

Time target – 5 minutes

To get the best practice, complete the summary before you read the discussion.

This practice involves a brief summary of one section of the reading.

READING PASSAGE

SPORT AND RECREATION

A large proportion of Australians, regardless of social position, income and age, participate in some form of sporting activity. The impact of sport extends over a wide range of associated activities in community and commercial fields. Sport is a large industry in Australia encompassing not only participants but also employment within the sporting infrastructure; manufacture of apparel, equipment and other goods (e.g. trophies); tourism and support industries (e.g. printing, media). The sporting activities of Australians include a range of organised and social sport, recreational and leisure activities undertaken both at home and away from home.

Involvement in sport

In March 1993, an ABS survey of persons 15 years of age and over was conducted throughout Australia to obtain information about involvement in sport during the previous 12 months. Involvement in sport was defined to include both paid and unpaid participation in playing and non-playing capacities. Spectator involvement in sport was excluded.

The survey found that one third of the Australian population aged 15 years and over were involved in sport, as players (3.1 million), non-players (0.5 million) or both players and non-players (0.9

million). More men than women were involved as players and as non-players.

Overall, 35% of males played sport compared to 23% of females, and at all ages a greater proportion of males than females played sport. Younger men and women were more likely to play sport than older men and women. Fifty-six per cent of men aged 15 to 24 played sport compared to 39% of women in the same age group. In the 25 to 34 age group 43% of men played sport, compared to 28% of women. Twenty per cent of men and 12% of women aged 65 and over played sport. For those involved in sport solely as non-players, the 35 to 44 years age group had the highest participation rate (8% for males, 9% for females). Their most common activities were as administrators or committee members.

Questions 1–8

Complete the summary of the first section of the Reading passage below. Choose your answers from the box below the summary.

Note: *There are more words than you will need to fill the gaps. You may use a word more than once if you wish.*

SUMMARY

In Australia, sport is not only a recreational and ..(1).. activity but also an industry. One survey looked at participation in sport based on whether participants were ..(2).. or ..(3).. and whether they were paid or not. The survey did not consider ..(4).. to be ..(5)..

In general, women were found to be ..(6).. involved in sport than men and there were ..(7).. young people involved than older people. The results of the survey also showed that ..(8).. were generally involved in two different capacities.

business	social	women
more	players	participants
less	non-players	most
fewer	unpaid	spectators

DISCUSSION

1   This sentence summarises the information in the first paragraph. The passage tells you that sport is important in two ways: as an activity and an industry. One kind of activity is already mentioned – 'recreational'. Note that this word is an adjective, therefore you need another adjective to complete the phrase. The possible answers must be either 'business', or 'social'. 'Business' is almost a synonym for 'industry', and therefore not appropriate for the answer. Therefore the answer is 'social'.

2, 3, 4 and 5   The sentence containing these questions is a summary of the second paragraph. The words, which must be nouns, that might be applicable are: 'players', 'non-players', 'women', 'participants' and 'spectators'. For Questions 2 and 3, you must put two types of participants. One of these could be 'women', but women are not mentioned at this point in the text. Therefore the only possibilities are 'players' and 'non-players'. It would not matter which you put first as it would still mean the same thing.

   The second part of this sentence, Questions 4 and 5, is a rephrasing of the last sentence of the paragraph. It includes the information left out of the last sentence, which a reader would be able to supply for him/herself. The complete meaning of that last sentence is: 'Spectator involvement in sport was excluded [from participation]'. Therefore, the answer to Question 4 is 'spectators'. By definition, spectators cannot be players, and spectators are automatically non-players. So neither of those words is possible for Question 5. The answer is 'participants'. In this case you cannot reverse the order of the answers as it would not make sense.

6 & 7   The sentence containing these two questions summarises the third paragraph of the reading. The structure of the sentence indicates that for Question 6 an adverb in the comparative form is needed and for Question 7 an adjective in the comparative is required. The possible words in the box are: 'more', 'less', 'fewer' and 'most'. The percentages of men and women in sport indicate that the answer for 6 is 'less' as it is the only adverb given which reflects those figures. The rest of the paragraph indicates that the numbers of young people involved in sport is greater than the number of older people involved; therefore the answer is 'more'. 'Most' is not possible as it is the superlative form, not the comparative.

8   This question summarises some of the information in the last paragraph about the activities on non-players. This paragraph tells you than non-players were involved 'as administrators or committee members'. Therefore the answer to this question is 'non-players'. This means that you have used this answer twice. Sometimes you have to use the same answer twice, although it is not common in the IELTS test.

EXERCISE 10

Time target – 5 minutes

This exercise is a summary of the last section of the Reading entitled 'Utilising Women's Skills'. For this exercise, we have put the summary and the answer choices first in order to encourage you to **read the summary first** and try to fill the gaps **without** referring to the reading.

Questions 1–6

Complete the summary for the last section of the Reading passage. Choose your answers from the box below the summary.

Note: *There are more word/phrases than you will need to fill the gaps. You may use a word more than once if you wish.*

SUMMARY

Two steps need to be taken for greater utilisation of women's expertise: ..(1).. of logistical supports and better ..(2).. of women into all industrial activities. These can be achieved by ..(3).. such facilities as child-care facilities and by ..(4).. a system of keeping women up-to-date when they are away from work ..(5).. It is also useful ..(6).. communication systems so that women can put forward their ideas.

to propose	integration	provision
adopting	providing	utilisation
adjusting	on holidays	for long periods
consider	to integrate	creation

READING PASSAGE

Effective Utilisation

9   In order to utilise female talents at all effectively, it may well be necessary, as many have already argued, to provide some simple logistical supports in the form of flexible work schedules, child-care facilities and the like. But it may be even more necessary to provide greater opportunity for working women in general and part-time workers in particular, to become integrated into the mainstream of organised activity.

10   This can occur only if industry then treats them as worthy of it, no matter whether they are "merely" part-time or whether they choose to take some time out to start a family. Some organisations, especially those facing a tight labour market, do provide such opportunities and do attempt to keep those on leave of absence in touch with policies and practices. They are probably too few for

comfort and too often stimulated by extremely short-sighted and short-lived motives. Unless these activities are integrated with the business strategy, they are unlikely to survive a slackening of the labour market or to give industry full benefit.

11 Finally, their potential is unlikely to be realised unless they are included in all the communication systems developed both to inform employees and to elicit their suggestions for improvement. Part-timers particularly, but also those who perform what have tradition-ally been regarded as women's jobs, are often excluded from these, so that their often unblinkered views are ignored.

Practice

Time target – 10 minutes

For this summary you have to find the words in the reading passage.

READING PASSAGE

A Under Pinochet, Chilean fruit exports boomed. The country has remained a major supplier of tem-perate fruits – grapes, nectarines, plums, peaches, pears and apples – to North America and Europe. More than 95 per cent of grape imports to the US are from Chile. Highly per-ishable exports prompted Cardoen Industries, better known for its weapons and explosives, to produce refrigerated containers for sea and air shipments. Almost all Chile's orchards are less than one hundred miles from a seaport. Over half of Chile's fruit exports are controlled by five transnational companies.

B Most of the estimated half a million jobs created by the fruit industry are temporary and sea-sonal. Over two-thirds of the labour force in Chile is now employed on a temporary basis, 60 per cent of whom work in the fruit sector.

C In the late 1980s in a major fruit-growing valley, temporary workers, employed for about three months of the year, were paid between $2 and $4 per day; one hectare (2.5 acres) of grapes in the valley earned the owner just under $5000.

D Many of these workers used to be smallholders or agricultural workers who were evicted from plots in Chile's central valley region to make way for commercial producers. Many temporary fruit workers migrate from north to south each year, following the peak moments in the harvest.

E Workers complain of crowded, squalid barracks and limited washing and sanitary facilities, crit-ical for those regularly exposed to pesticides. Imports of pesticides increased more than eight-fold between 1976 and 1986. Some 80 per cent of workers in the fruit industry say the problem of health was either "very serious" or "serious".

Questions 1–8

*Complete the summary below. Choose **ONE** word from the passage for each answer.*

SUMMARY

Chilean fruit exports, which are grown in ..(1).. not far from the coast, are sent mainly to North America and Europe in ..(2).. Most workers have only ..(3).. work. Many of the poorly-paid workers were ..(4).. from their own land and need to ..(5).. to wherever harvesting is at a ..(6).. Living conditions for these workers are ..(7).. with limited facilities essential for workers who are exposed to other ..(8).. health hazards such as pesticides.

DISCUSSION

This type of summary question is generally slightly more difficult than the ones where you are given answer choices in a box. One of the difficulties is that the word(s) you need may not be exactly where you expect to find them. You may have to look for them throughout the reading.

1   You might guess the answer for this one if you know that an orchard is where fruit is grown. However, to find the correct word in the reading, you must read all of Paragraph **A** and connect the fruit exports in the first sentence with the orchards in the second last sentence.

2   For Question 2 you also have to search Paragraph **A** for something that fruit can **be sent in**. After 'in' you need a noun, and you know that fruit goes bad quickly, so the answer is in the sentence 'Highly perishable exports prompted Cardoen Industries, ..., to produce refrigerated containers for sea and air shipments'. The question asks for only one word, so the correct answer is 'containers'. It is important that you write this answer in the plural, as the singular would require an article and also it would not be logical to have only one container.

3   Paragraph **B** tells you that jobs are 'temporary and seasonal'. Question 3 paraphrases this information. Therefore the answer is either word, 'temporary' or 'seasonal'. It does not matter which you put. Either will be counted correct.

4   The information in this sentence summarises both Paragraphs **C** and **D**. However, all the words you need can be found in Paragraph **D**. 'The workers used to be smallholders ... who were evicted from plots' has the same meaning as 'the ... workers have been evicted from their own land'. So the answer is 'evicted'. You must have the 'ed' ending on the word to be scored correct.

5 & 6   The second half of this same sentence is a paraphrase and shortening of the last sentence in Paragraph **D**. The correct answers are 'migrate' and 'peak'. 'Migrate' must be in this form as it is part of an infinitive.

7   This question requires you to know or guess that 'barracks' is where people live in groups. The passage tells you that the barracks are crowded and squalid. It doesn't matter whether you know what squalid means or not. The grammar tells you it is an adjective describing the barracks, or the place where the workers live. So you can give either adjective for your answer: 'crowded' or 'squalid'.

8   The position of this question in the sentence should tell you that you need an adjective. It is quite clear from the text that a pesticide constitutes a health hazard and the best adjective you can find in the reading for the kind of health hazard is 'serious'. The answer is 'serious'.

EXERCISE 11

Time target – 10 minutes

For this exercise, go back to the reading for Exercise 5, 'Training' (p. 42).

Questions 1–7

*Complete the summary notes using **ONE** or **TWO** words from the passage for each note.*

SUMMARY NOTES

- Training is a prominent activity in labour reform
- Focus of a Training Expenditure Survey was on employee training time and ..**(1)**..
- Essentials of formal training were found to be the existence of a ..**(2)**.. and a format for developing skills related to the ..**(3)**..
- Reasons for providing training are to improve ..**(4)**.., facilitate career development and increase the range of skills of ..**(5)**..
- Constraints on training consisted of ..**(6)**.. and ..**(7)**..

EXERCISE 12

Time target – 7 minutes

For this exercise, go back to the reading in Exercise 9, 'The Changing Nature Of Careers' (p. 63).

Questions 1–11

*Complete the summary using **NO MORE THAN THREE** words taken from the reading.*

SUMMARY

Vertical movement is defined as a ..(1).. involving promotion up a ..(2)... Both speed and timing of vertical movement vary and today there are ..(3).. for vertical movement.

A change in ..(4).. function or field of work is called horizontal movement. Individuals often find that further study or ..(5).. may be necessary in order to learn new skills and acquire new types of expertise. Two reasons for making a horizontal career change are to obtain greater ..(6).. and/or to facilitate further ..(7)...

Sometimes vertical movement is associated with ..(8).., in which a person is transferred to a branch or affiliate. This movement away from the ..(9).. base involves both distance and level of ..(10)...

Whichever type of movement a person experiences, she or he will undergo a process of ..(11).. before they are ready for the next career change.

EXERCISE 13

Time target – 7 minutes

For this exercise go back to the practice reading for viewpoint questions, 'A Woman's Work is Never Done' (p. 55).

Questions 1–7

Complete the summary. Choose your answers from the words in the box below the summary.

SUMMARY

The social and personal ..(1).. women have made by entering the ..(2).. must be offset against the losses. While they may have won greater freedom, their high level of ..(3).. in the ..(4).. has left them at a disadvantage. They do not have the ..(5).. of men in full-time employment. ..(6).., they are further disadvantaged because of their inescapable ..(7).. obligations.

domestic	paid labour force	children
trading	official job market	informal labour sector
bargaining power	salaries	losses
obligations	freedom	gains
global market place	nowadays	furthermore
however		

To complete this section on summarising questions, do Reading Passage 3 from Practice test 1 (p. 13) again. Try to complete it in 15 minutes. Then you can check your answers in the Answer Key.

Make a copy of the Reading answer sheet on page 172 to write your answers on.

IELTS PRACTICE TEST 2

READING

TIME ALLOWED: 1 hour

NUMBER OF QUESTIONS: 42

Instructions

All answers must be written on the answer sheet

The test is divided as follows:

Reading Passage 1	*Questions 1–16*
Reading Passage 2	*Questions 17–32*
Reading Passage 3	*Questions 33–42*

Start at the beginning of the test and work through it. You should answer all the questions.

If you cannot do a particular question leave it and go on to the next. You can return to it later.

READING PASSAGE 1

You should spend about 20 minutes on Questions 1–16 which are based on Reading Passage 1 on pages 3 and 4.

Questions 1–6

*Reading Passage 1 has 7 sections A–G. Choose the most suitable heading for each section from the list of headings below. Write the appropriate numbers (**i–x**) in boxes 1–6 on your answer sheet.*

Note: *There are more headings than sections so you will not use all of them. You may use any of the headings more than once.*

Example	Answer
C	**iv**

HEADINGS

(i)	Daniel Defoe wrote *Robinson Crusoe*
(ii)	Australian culture and *The Bulletin*
(iii)	Magazines in Australia today
(iv)	Australia's first magazine
(v)	The first magazines
(vi)	Australians depend on England for news
(vii)	Historical value of magazines
(viii)	Improvements in printing technology
(ix)	Printing of photographs
(x)	Some magazines have died

Questions 1–6

1	Section **A**		**4**	Section **E**
2	Section **B**		**5**	Section **F**
3	Section **D**		**6**	Section **G**

AUSTRALIAN POPULAR MAGAZINES

A The magazine as a product for leisure reading, enjoyment and information, or, as the Gentlemen of the day would have put it 'edification', had its origins in England during the early years of the eighteenth century where the innovator was Daniel Defoe, the writer of *Robinson Crusoe*. The word magazine comes from the French *magasin* which originally meant a storehouse, an apt term since the first printed magazines were holdings for a miscellany of writings on various subjects. Defoe titled his magazine *The Review*, which, five years after the first issue, was followed by two other now famous magazines *The Tatler* and *The Spectator* both publications founded by the same partner-writers Richard Steele and Joseph Addison.

B As for Australian popular magazines, initially, during the founding days of the colonies, readers at the time depended on the slow sailing ships from 'home' to bring them, among the other necessary items, newspapers and journals.

C It was not until 1855 that Australia produced its own, and first popular magazine. This was the highly successful *Melbourne Punch*, which had a life span reaching into the first quarter of the twentieth century.

D Popular illustrated magazines rapidly became an important and significant factor to the literate in Australia, who were forming our national image, as were the singers of ballads and strolling entertainers who were also making a major contribution. Out of this background the now famous old *Bulletin* emerged in 1880. From the start *The Bulletin* policy was to foster and encourage Australian writers and artists: it succeeded in making the names and reputations of Henry Lawson, 'Banjo' Paterson, Steele Rudd and scores of others. It created a new, unique school of black-and-white art which, for instance, gave Phil May his big chance and eventual world recognition. The influence of *The Bulletin* was such that this era of the legendary 'nineties' is regarded as the source of our national culture.

From this Australian pre-Federation era a number of fascinating magazines were not only founded, but many were originated and owned by distinguished writers of the day. These included the writers Henry Kendall, Marcus Clarke, Rolf Boldrewood, Randolph Bedford, Edward Dyson, Norman Lindsay and C. J. Dennis among others.

E As they were developed technical advances were promptly exploited, the most sensational being the development of photo-process engraving which allowed, for the first time, the reproduction of 'half-tone' photographs. This ingenious method simply required a photograph to be re-photographed through a dotted glass screen on to a metal sheet where, after an acid bath, the tones are simulated by a pattern of minute, raised dots varying in size. When inked the metal sheet is ready for reproducing a facsimile photograph made of tiny dots. Previously, a scene or an event was drawn in reverse, or back to front, by an artist on to a prepared block of wood. This was then given to an engraver who, with a variety of delicate cutting tools, would gouge away areas of the drawing leaving a raised surface which, when inked and pressure applied would give a black and white impression of the image. And for the first time too photo-engraving enabled an artist to draw a cartoon, for instance, in any manner or style he chose and the printed result, which could now be enlarged or reduced in size, would be accurate in every detail just as it was drawn.

Other not so significant technical developments have been high-speed printing presses, simultaneous multi-colour printing, and certain electronic 'scanner' equipment for preparing colour illustrations.

F By and large contemporary Australian magazines today do not differ greatly in content from those of the last century. There are some new directions: the high political content of *The Bulletin* for instance, reflects an awareness that Australia is increasingly being drawn into the wider international community – the features and articles about 'Big Business', home and overseas reflect this appreciation.

Whilst some one-time popular and very successful magazines – *Pix* and the original *People* for example – have not survived the years following World War II into the 1980s, the long running *Australasian Post* has managed not only to survive for 120 years (with a slight name change in 1946) but the magazine has been, for quite some time now, heading the list of the largest circulation for an Australian magazine of its kind. A large part of this success has resulted from a conscious editorial policy of an emphasis on Australiana. Other contemporary magazines like the Australian *Penthouse* and *Playboy*, *Cleo* and *Cosmopolitan* – there are others – have no policy to pursue national identity, but rather to embrace an international quality or, in the case of *Penthouse*, some other point of interest.

G Today, at a time of renewed national assessment, publications of the past that may have seemed inconsequential assume fresh importance as a source for the broad study of our culture. The changes in social behaviour, tastes, attitudes, fashion and manners which they reflect have become a large part of our conception of ourselves.

Questions 7–11

Look at Questions 7–11.

Classify the following as belonging to:

    N   *New method of printing illustrations*

    O   *Old method of printing illustrations*

    B   *Both methods of printing illustrations*

Write the appropriate letters in boxes 7–11 on your answer sheet.

  7 a wooden block

  8 a metal sheet

  9 a glass screen

10 inking

11 image is reversed

Questions 12–16

Several magazine titles are mentioned in Reading Passage 1. For which magazines are the following statements true?

*Write the name of **ONE** appropriate magazine for each question in boxes 12–16 on your answer sheet.*

Example	*Answer*
The first magazine	**The Review**

12 is no longer published

13 the first Australian magazine

14 has a strong political focus

15 has changed its name

16 does not emphasise Australiana

READING PASSAGE 2

You should spend about 20 minutes on Questions 17–32 which are based on Reading Passage 2 on pages 7 and 8.

Questions 17–20

Reading Passage 2 has 5 sections A–E.

*From the list of headings below choose the most suitable heading for sections **B** to **E**.*

*Write the appropriate numbers (**i–viii**) in boxes 17–20 on your answer sheet.*

Note: *There are more headings than sections so you will not use all of them. You may use any of the headings more than once.*

HEADINGS

(i)   Cells affected by radiation

(ii)   Effects of low-dose radiation

(iii)   Effects on cell multiplication

(iv)   Effects of radiation on cells

(v)   Sources of radiation

(vi)   Radiation in the food chain

(vii)   Dissemination of radiation

(viii) Health effects of radiation

Example	*Answer*
Section A	**v**

17   Section B

18   Section C

19   Section D

20   Section E

RADIATION AND HUMAN HEALTH

A Radioactivity occurs naturally. The main source comes from natural sources in space, rocks, soil, water and even the human body itself. This is called background radiation and levels vary from place to place, though the average dose is fairly constant. The radiation which is of most concern is artificial radiation which results from human activities. Sources of this include the medical use of radioactive materials, fallout and contamination from nuclear bomb tests, discharges from the nuclear industry, and the storage and dumping of radioactive waste.

B While artificial radiation accounts for a small proportion of the total, its effects can be disproportionate. Some of the radioactive materials discharged by human activity are not found in nature, such as plutonium, while others which are found naturally may be discharged in different physical and chemical forms, allowing them to spread more readily into the environment, or perhaps accumulate in the food-chain.

For all these reasons, simple comparisons of background and artificial radioactivity may not reflect the relative hazards. Equally important, it has never been shown that there is such a thing as a safe dose of radiation and so the fact that we are progressively raising global levels should be of as much concern to us as the possibility of another major nuclear disaster like Chernobyl. Every nuclear test, nuclear reactor or shipment of plutonium means an additional and unnecessary health risk.

C In general, the effects of radiation can be divided into those which affect the individuals exposed and those which affect their descendants. Somatic effects are those which appear in the irradiated or exposed individual. These include cancer and leukaemia. Hereditary or genetic effects are those which arise in subsequent generations.

Many of the elements which our bodies need are produced by the nuclear industry as radioactive isotopes or variants. Some of these are released into the environment, for example iodine and carbon, two common elements used by our bodies. Our bodies do not know the difference between an element which is radioactive and one which is not. So radioactive elements can be absorbed into living tissues, bones or the blood, where they continue to give off radiation. Radioactive strontium behaves like calcium – an essential ingredient in our bones – in our bodies. Strontium deposits in the bones send radioactivity into the bone marrow, where the blood cells are formed, causing leukemia.

D There are three principal effects which radiation can have on cells: firstly the cell may be killed; secondly the way the cell multiplies may be affected, resulting in cancer; and thirdly damage may occur in the cells of the ovaries or testes, leading to the development of a child with an inherited abnormality.

In most cases, cell death only becomes significant when large numbers of cells are killed, and the effects of cell death therefore only become apparent at comparatively high dose levels. If a damaged cell is able to survive a radiation dose, the situation is different. In many cases the effect of the cell damage may never become apparent. A few malfunctioning cells will not significantly affect an organ where the large majority are still behaving normally.

However, if the affected cell is a germ cell within the ovaries or testes, the situation is different. Ionising radiation can damage DNA, the molecule which acts as the cell's 'instruction book'. If that germ cell later forms a child, all of the child's cells will carry the same defect. The localised chemical alteration of DNA in a single cell may be expressed as an inherited abnormality in one or many future generations.

In the same way that a somatic cell in body tissue is changed in such a way that it or its descendants escape the control processes which normally control cell replication, the group of cells formed may continue to have a selective advantage in growth over surrounding tissue. It may ultimately increase sufficiently in size to form a detectable cancer and in some cases cause death by spreading locally or to other parts of the body.

E While there is now broad agreement about the effects of high-level radiation, there is controversy over the long-term effect of low-level doses. This is complicated by the length of time it takes for effects to show up, the fact that the populations being studied (bomb survivors, people exposed to nuclear tests or workers in the nuclear industry) are small and exact doses are hard to calculate.

All that can be said is that predictions made about the effects of a given dose vary. A growing number of scientists point to evidence that there is a disproportionately high risk from low doses of radiation. Others assume a directly proportionate link between the received dose and the risk of cancer for all levels of dose, while there are some who claim that at low doses there is a disproportionately low level of risk.

Questions 21–26

Classify the following as linked in the passage to:

> **BR**   **B**ackground **R**adiation
>
> **AR**   **A**rtificial **R**adiation
>
> **N**   Neither
>
> or **B**   **B**oth

Write the appropriate letters in boxes 21–26 on your answer sheet.

21 produced by the human body

22 involves only safe amounts of radiation

23 is used for medical purposes

24 includes plutonium

25 produces a constant level of radiation

26 can enter the food chain

Questions 27–32

Complete the summary of Section D of Reading Passage 1 below. Choose your answers from the box below the summary and write them in boxes 27–32 on your answer sheet.

Note: *There are more words/phrases than you will need to fill the gaps. You may use a word or phrase more than once if you wish.*

SUMMARY

Radiation can affect an organism by damaging ..**(27)**.. which may then die or malfunction. If the ..**(28)**.. affected in this way is small, the effect will not be too drastic and may not be noticeable. Alternatively, the ..**(29)**.. may grow uncontrollably and form cancers, in which case the organism is likely to die.

If the DNA in a germ cell in the ovaries or testes is affected, any ..**(30)**.. originating from that ..**(31)**.. may display ..**(32)**.., which can in turn be passed on to further offspring.

offspring	damaged cells
further offspring	individual cells
organisms	number of cells
cancers	germ cell
abnormalities	DNA

READING PASSAGE 3

You should spend about 20 minutes on Questions 33–42 which are based on Reading Passage 3 on pages 10 and 11.

ASIA'S ENERGY TEMPTATION

Nuclear power supplies 5% of the world's energy from more than 400 plants. But with the exception of France and Japan, the rich world has stopped ordering new reactors. A technology that was once deemed both clean and "too cheap to metre" has proved to be neither. The industry's chief hope now rests on the poor world. Western firms with reactors to sell will be relying on Asia, where electricity demand is growing at 8% a year. New reactors are planned in China, Taiwan, Indonesia, South Korea, Pakistan and India. It is good news for the reactors' vendors; but these countries are making a mistake.

The economic arguments for building new nuclear plants are flawed. The marginal costs of generating electricity from nuclear energy may be tiny, but, as the technology now stands, huge and uncertain costs are involved in building the power stations, dealing with spent fuel, and decommissioning. Many western governments which sang nuclear's praises now admit that gas and hydropower can produce cheaper electricity.

The economics of nuclear power in the poor world could prove to be worse still. As in the rich world, fossil fuels such as gas and coal are invariably cheaper. In China the case for nuclear power may be a little stronger as domestic reserves of coal – though huge – are located far from some areas of growing electricity demand. But most developing countries, including China, are strapped for cash and need to increase electricity supply quickly to meet soaring demand. Nuclear plants fail on both counts: they are hugely capital-intensive, and can take as long as ten years to build.

Those still charmed by nuclear power nowadays make three new arguments in its favour: that it is a defence against climate change, against another OPEC-administered oil shock, and against the inevitable exhaustion of fossil fuels. None bears close examination.

At present rates of demand, the world has enough oil to last for more than 40 years, enough gas for more than 60 years and enough coal for more than 230 years. Naturally, demand will increase; but so will reserves as companies explore more widely and costs fall. Since 1970 viable reserves of oil have almost doubled while those of gas have leapt three-fold. One distant day a crunch will come, but as it approaches fossil-fuel prices will rise, making alternative forms of energy, perhaps including nuclear power, competitive. That is no reason to spend on nuclear now.

An oil shock is a more worrying prospect, despite today's low oil price and OPEC's present inability to budge it upwards. After all, the cartel still sits on 75% of the world's economically viable reserves, and the politics of the Middle East can change at a stroke. However, even if an oil shock is a real danger, building nuclear reactors is not a good way to avert it. A higher oil price would have a relatively small effect on the supply of electricity – the only sort of energy that nuclear power can now provide. Just over a tenth of the world's electricity (and 14% of Asia's) is generated from oil, and the proportion has fallen steadily since 1970.

Besides, there are superior, non-nuclear, ways to prepare for an oil shock. Governments could take advantage of today's low oil prices to build up their stocks. Especially where congestion and pollution are serious problems, they could try to restrict the growth of car use, or promote cars which guzzle less fuel. For governments keen to reduce electricity's remaining dependence on oil still further, there are usually cheaper alternatives to nuclear, such as coal or hydropower.

Climate change is a legitimate worry. Although still riddled with uncertainties, the science of climate change is becoming firmer: put too much carbon in the atmosphere and you might end up cooking the earth, with possibly catastrophic results. But here again, switching immediately to nuclear power is not the best response. Cutting the hefty subsidies that go to the world's coal producers would help tilt the world's energy balance towards natural gas, which gives off much less carbon dioxide. Developing countries subsidise electricity prices to the tune of up to $120 billion a year, according to World Bank estimates. If prices reflected the true costs of generation, electricity demand would fall, thus cutting greenhouse emissions.

Once the tough job of cutting subsidies is over, governments might want to reduce greenhouse gases further. Again there are carbon-free energies that merit more subsidies than nuclear. The costs of many renewable technologies, such as solar and wind power, have fallen dramatically in recent decades.

Moreover, supporting nuclear power to ward off climate change means swapping one environmental risk for another. Voters in many countries fear radiation like the plague. The risks of nuclear accidents may be tiny, but when they happen they can be catastrophic. Renewables are not without their environmental disadvantages (wind turbines, for example, can be unsightly on hilltops), but are much cleaner than nuclear. The billions rich countries each year pump into nuclear research would be better spent on renewables instead.

Having been invented, nuclear power will not disappear. The nuclear industry still has a job to do, running existing nuclear plants to the end of their lives as cheaply and safely as possible. For now, the case for nuclear power is full of holes. Asia should resist the temptation to throw its money into them.

Questions 33–36

*Look at the following lists of **CAUSES**, A–F and **EFFECTS**, Questions 33–36.*

*Match each **EFFECT** with its **CAUSE**.*

Write your answers in boxes 33–36 on your answer sheet.

Note: *There are more causes than effects so you will not have to use all of them. You may use any cause more than once.*

Example	*Answer*
prices rise	**A**

EFFECTS

33 the supply of electricity is hardly affected

34 oil can be stockpiled

35 less electricity is used

36 more natural gas is used

CAUSES

A reserves of fossil fuels go down

B reserves of fossil fuels increase

C oil prices are low

D electric subsidies are reduced

E coal subsidies are reduced

F demand for fossil fuels increases

G oil prices are high

Questions 37–42

Using **NO MORE THAN THREE WORDS**, *complete the following statements. Write your answers in boxes 37–42 on your answer sheet.*

37 Nuclear power plants require a great deal of ..... to build.

38 The main environmental risk attached to nuclear power is .....

39 Two carbon-free forms of energy are ..... and .....

40 Money presently used for nuclear research could be better spent on .....

41 One disadvantage of ..... is that they spoil the landscape.

42 The nuclear industry should operate nuclear power plants .....

Make a copy of the Reading answer sheet on page 172 to write your answers on.

IELTS PRACTICE TEST 3

READING

TIME ALLOWED: 1 hour

NUMBER OF QUESTIONS: 39

Instructions

All answers must be written on the answer sheet

The test is divided as follows:

Reading Passage 1	*Questions 1–14*
Reading Passage 2	*Questions 15–28*
Reading Passage 3	*Questions 29–39*

Start at the beginning of the test and work through it. You should answer all the questions.

If you cannot do a particular question leave it and go on to the next. You can return to it later.

READING PASSAGE 1

You should spend about 20 minutes on Questions 1–14 which are based on Reading Passage 1 on pages 2 and 3.

NEW-AGE TRANSPORT

Computerised design, advanced materials and new technologies are being used to produce machines of a type never seen before.

It looks as if it came straight from the set of *Star Wars*. It has four-wheel drive and rises above rocky surfaces. It lowers and raises its nose when going up and down hills. And when it comes to a river, it turns amphibious: two hydrojets power it along by blasting water under its body. There is room for two passengers and a driver, who sit inside a glass bubble operating electronic, aircraft-type controls. A vehicle so daring on land and water needs windscreen wipers – but it doesn't have any. Water molecules are disintegrated on the screen's surface by ultrasonic sensors.

This unusual vehicle is the Racoon. It is an invention not of Hollywood but of Renault, a rather conservative French state-owned carmaker, better known for its family hatchbacks. Renault built the Racoon to explore new freedoms for designers and engineers created by advances in materials and manufacturing processes. Renault is thinking about startlingly different cars; other producers have radical new ideas for trains, boats and aeroplanes.

The first of the new freedoms is in design. Powerful computer-aided design (CAD) systems can replace with a click of a computer mouse hours of laborious work done on thousands of drawing boards. So new products, no matter how complicated, can be developed much faster. For the first time, Boeing will not have to build a giant replica of its new airliner, the 777, to make sure all the bits fit together. Its CAD system will take care of that.

But Renault is taking CAD further. It claims the Racoon is the world's first vehicle to be designed within the digitised world of virtual reality. Complex programs were used to simulate the vehicle and the terrain that it was expected to cross. This allowed a team led by Patrick Le Quement, Renault's industrial-design director, to "drive" it long before a prototype existed.

Renault is not alone in thinking that virtual reality will transform automotive design. In Detroit, Ford is also investigating its potential. Jack Telnac, the firm's head of design, would like designers in different parts of the world to work more closely together, linked by computers. They would do more than style cars. Virtual reality will allow engineers to peer inside the working parts of a vehicle. Designers will watch bearings move, oil flow, gears mesh and hydraulics pump. As these techniques catch on, even stranger vehicles are likely to come along.

Transforming these creations from virtual reality to actual reality will also become easier, especially with advances in materials. Firms that once bashed everything out of steel now find that new alloys or composite materials (which can be made from mixtures of plastic, resin, ceramics and metals, reinforced with fibres such as glass or carbon) are changing the rules of manufacturing. At the same time, old materials keep getting better, as their producers try to secure their place in the factory of the future. This competition is increasing the pace of development of all materials.

One company in this field is Scaled Composites. It was started in 1982 by Burt Rutan, an aviator who has devised many unusual aircraft. His company develops and tests prototypes that have ranged from business aircraft to air racers. It has also worked on composite sails for the America's Cup yacht race and on General Motors' Ultralite, a 100-miles-per-gallon experimental family car built from carbon fibre.

Again, the Racoon reflects this race between the old and the new. It uses conventional steel and what Renault describes as a new "high-limit elastic steel" in its chassis. This steel is 30% lighter than the usual kind. The Racoon also has parts made from composites. Renault plans to replace the petrol engine with a small gas turbine, which could be made from heat-resisting ceramics, and use it to run a generator that would provide power for electric motors at each wheel.

With composites it is possible to build many different parts into a single component. Fiat, Italy's biggest car maker, has worked out that it could reduce the number of components needed in one of its car bodies from 150 to 16 by using a composite shell rather than one made of steel. Aircraft and cars may increasingly be assembled as if they were plastic kits.

Advances in engine technology also make cars lighter. The Ultralite, which Scaled Composites helped to design for General Motors, uses a two-stroke engine in a "power pod" at the rear of the vehicle. The engine has been developed from an East German design and weighs 40% less than a conventional engine but produces as much power. It is expected to run cleanly enough to qualify as an ultra-low emissions vehicle under California's tough new rules.

Questions 1–5

*Choose the appropriate letters **A–D** for each question and write them in boxes 1-5 on your answer sheet.*

1 How does the Racoon cross water?

    A It swims.

    B It raises its nose.

    C It uses hydrojets.

    D It uses its four-wheel drive.

2 What is Renault most famous for?

    A startlingly different cars

    B family cars

    C advances in design

    D boat and train design

3 Why will Boeing not need a replica of the 777?

    A It can use computers to check the design.

    B It already has enough experience with plans.

    C It will only need to upgrade the replica of the previous model.

    D It can make sure all the bits fit together.

4 How did Renault test drive the Racoon?

    A over rocky terrain

    B in actual reality

    C over French country roads

    D in virtual reality

5 Which of the following is **NOT** mentioned as an ingredient of a composite?

    A oil

    B resin

    C glass

    D steel

Questions 6–8

Using **NO MORE THAN THREE WORDS**, *complete the following statements. Write your answers in boxes 6–8 on your answer sheet.*

6 One future design feature of the Racoon might be a …

7 In the future cars might be put together like …

8 The advantage of the Ultralite engine is that it is 40% … than other car engines.

Questions 9–14

These five companies are mentioned in Reading Passage 1. Which company is each of the following design features associated with?

Write the letters for the appropriate company in boxes 9–14 on your answer sheet.

> **SC** *if it is* **Scaled Composites**
>
> **R** *if it is* **Renault**
>
> **GM** *if it is* **General Motors**
>
> **F** *if it is* **Fiat**
>
> **B** *if it is* **Boeing**

9 a power pod

10 electronic controls

11 a composite body

12 elastic steel

13 aircraft prototypes

14 ultrasonic sensors

READING PASSAGE 2

You should spend about 20 minutes on Questions 15–28 which are based on Reading Passage 2 on pages 6 and 7.

GETTING GIRLS ON-LINE

When Nancy Leveson, now a computer science professor at the University of Washington, was teaching math at a California high school, her best student also happened to be one of the prettiest and most popular girls around. And when the girl got the highest score on a test, Leveson thought nothing of announcing the achievement while handing back the papers. As soon as the class ended, though, the distraught student approached. She begged her teacher never, *ever* to embarrass her like that again.

The incident happened nearly 20 years ago, but Leveson notes that little has changed. Now, as then, too many teenage girls feel uncomfortable and even unwelcome in the realms of math, science and computing. Research shows that girls who are gifted in these subjects in elementary school begin to shy away from them by the seventh grade. Eventually, they convince themselves that these are male domains. "By saying only men are good at these things, you make the women who are good at them seem like freaks," says Leveson.

Increasingly, however, educators are trying to reverse the process by retraining teachers and redirecting students. Funded with more than $1 million by the National Science Foundation (NSF) and seven corporations, Computer Equity Expert Project (CEEP) showed 200 math and computer-science teachers how to recognise and eliminate gender bias in their classrooms. CEEP urged teachers to bring more girls into the world of computers by setting up mentoring programs with older students and having girls-only days at the school computer labs.

Both public and private schools are trying to close the technology gap. Because girls tend to do better in the sciences without the distraction of boys, three California schools have started girls-only math classes over the last two years, with promising results. Other schools are hooking up with colleges for help and inspiration.

But however wonderful the subject looks in high school, interest often diminishes in college, where women earned only 30% of the undergraduate degrees awarded in computer science in 1991, and 16% in engineering in 1993, as opposed to medical school, where women make up 36% of total enrolment. The proportion shrinks still more at the doctoral level, where women receive only 15% of computer science PhDs and under 10% of engineering PhDs.

Many college women are turned off by the macho swagger of technojocks at schools like MIT, where staying awake for three days to perfect a piece of software is seen as a test of virility. That kind of attitude "sets cultural parameters not just for MIT but for the intense nature of the computer culture everywhere," says Steven Levy, author of *Hackers: Heroes of the Computer Revolution.* As a result, it's hard to find female role models in computer science.

To keep women interested in the field, Nancy Leveson and a colleague from the University of British Columbia spearheaded a program that will match 20 female undergraduates with faculty mentors around the country this summer, thanks to a $240 000 grant from the NSF.

In Rochester, NY, the Rochester Institute of Technology's Women in Science, Engineering and Math mentoring program aims to spark high school girls' career interests by linking 140 girls and professional women in a computer network. Coordinators, who hope to extend the four-month program to three years, note the intense interest shown by girls and women. "I can't keep the mentors away," says Carol O'Leary, who helped set the program up. "I was looking for 40, and I have 67. Women are anxious to give of themselves."

Eventually, these computer educators would like to make gender-specific programs obsolete, but that will happen only when computer-science education becomes more creative, according to Paula Rayman, director of Pathways for Women in the Sciences, a research program at Wellesley College. By way of example, Rayman points to her 9-year-old daughter, Lily, whose fourth-grade class at the Bowman Elementary School in Lexington, Mass., is learning *several* sciences under the guise of bicycle repair. The kids aren't just fixing bikes but ingesting knowledge about mechanics, scientific history and the physics of motion. They're also using their computers to generate charts, graphs and databases. Children of both sexes are eager to work with computers because the machines are revealed as both entertaining and useful, not just as a source of boring drills or violent games, which girls usually find unappealing.

"When it comes to girls and computers," says Rayman, "we've found that there are three ingredients for user-friendliness: hands-on experience, teamwork and relevance." These ingredients, of course, would increase anyone's mastery of computers, as well as the usefulness of the machines. By trying to do a better job of teaching girls, computer scientists may learn quite a lot themselves.

Questions 15–18

*Choose the appropriate letters **A–D** for each question and write them in boxes 15–18 on your answer sheet.*

15 Nancy Leveson is

    A the girl who got the highest score on a test

    B a university professor

    C a high school teacher of math

    D one of the prettiest girls in school

16 Females generally do best at math and science

    A up to seventh grade

    B when they feel comfortable and welcome in the course

    C when they are teenagers

    D when they can compete with males

17 CEEP is

    A providing funds for teacher training

    B redirecting students

    C banning boys from the computer labs

    D helping more girls study computers

18 Which of the following is true about women studying in university?

    A 10% studying engineering got PhDs

    B 36% of total enrolments are in medical school

    C 16% of undergraduate engineering degrees were awarded to women

    D 30% studying computer science in 1991 got degrees

Questions 19–22

Four individuals are mentioned in Reading Passage 2. For whom are the following statements true?

Write the appropriate letters in boxes 19–22 on your answer sheet.

   NL   *Nancy Leveson*   **SL**   *Steve Levy*

   PR   *Paula Rayman*   **CO**   *Carol O'Leary*

Example	*Answer*
Used to teach mathematics	**NL**

19 has a daughter

20 helped organise the mentor program

21 wrote a book

22 is head of the mentor program

Questions 23–28

Do the following statements reflect the claims of the writer in Reading Passage 2?

In boxes 23–28 on your answer sheet write:

   YES   *if the statement agrees with the writer*

   NO   *if the statement contradicts the writer*

   NOT GIVEN   *if it is impossible to say what the writer thinks about this*

23 The overwhelmingly male computer culture repels many women.

24 The Rochester Institute of Technology is organising a three-year mentoring program for girls.

25 Special computer programs are being written for women.

26 Women are often anxious about themselves.

27 Physics and history are two of the main subjects taught at Bowman.

28 Computer scientists are likely to learn a lot from teaching girls.

READING PASSAGE 3

You should spend about 20 minutes on Questions 29–39 which are based on Reading Passage 3 on pages 11 and 12.

Questions 29–33

Reading Passage 3 has 8 sections A–H.

*Choose the most suitable heading for sections **C–F** and **H** from the list of headings below. Write the appropriate numbers (**i–ix**) in boxes 29–33 on your answer sheet.*

Note: *There are more headings than sections so you will not use all of them. You may use any of the headings more than once.*

HEADINGS

(i)   Rational city planning

(ii)   Family housing

(iii)   Parking facilities in the city

(iv)   Profit-making housing developments

(v)   Parking your car

(vi)   Cities for people?

(vii)   Appropriate living space

(viii)   High density accommodation in cities

(ix)   Housing as a business

Example	*Answer*
Section A	**vi**

29   Section C

30   Section D

31   Section E

32   Section F

33   Section H

DO WE NEED CITIES ANY MORE?

A I don't want to live in a city. Perhaps we divide naturally into two types: those for whom cities are vibrant and exciting, a focus for human activity; and those for whom they are dirty, noisy and dangerous. It may be unfashionable, but I'm in the latter camp. I do not believe that we are a species whose behaviour improves in overcrowded conditions.

B A new study proposes a significant increase in the capacity of towns and cities through a combination of increased housing densities, lower on-plot provision for cars and more on-street parking, and the re-use of marginal open space that is 'devoid of any amenity value'. The benefit of this approach is to reduce the loss of green fields and to help 'move towards more sustainable patterns of development'.

C This study suggests that it would be possible to achieve a 25% increase in density in a typical provincial city without changing the traditional street scene, although it would be necessary to reduce the size of the houses and substitute parking spaces for garages. Therefore, the cost of this approach is to have more people living in smaller homes at higher densities, along streets that are lined with parked cars. Can we really accept the notion that space within dwellings may be reduced even further? In times when, we are told, living standards are rising in real terms, is it realistic to seek to reduce personal space standards?

D The streets of many inner suburbs are already lined with cars on both sides, reducing movement to a single lane. Increasing densities means accepting urban streets that are designed as linear car parks, bounded by even smaller living units and tempered only by occasional trees sprouting from the tarmac. Would the benefits of higher density be worth the disadvantages of increasing on-street parking? Can we achieve a satisfactory visual environment from such raw materials? Higher urban densities may be communally good for us, but they will fail to meet the aspirations of many prospective home owners.

E Those without economic choice can be directed to live in this way, but if we are to continue to rely on the private sector to produce this urban housing, it will need to appeal to the private developers' customers. Who will choose to live in these high-density developments of small dwellings, with minimal open space and a chance to park on the highway if you are lucky enough to find a space? The main consumers will be single people, couples without children, and perhaps some 'empty nesters' (people whose children have grown up and left home). These are people who can choose to spend much of their time outside their home, making the most of those urban cultural opportunities or getting away at weekends to a country cottage or sporting activities.

F The combination of a young family and a mortgage restricts the mobility and spending power of many couples. Most people with a family will try to avoid bringing up their children in a cramped flat or house. Space for independent activity is important in developing the individual and in maintaining family equilibrium. The garden is the secure place where the children can work off excess energy.

G There is a danger that planners may take a dispassionate, logical view of how we should live, and seek to force society into that mould. A few years ago a European Commission study provided a good example of this. It took the view, quite sensibly, that housing should not be under-occupied because this is a waste of resources. Therefore, it would be much better if the many thousands of old ladies who live alone in large detached houses would move into small urban flats, thus releasing the large houses for families. What the study failed to recognise was that many of those old ladies prefer to continue to live in their family home with their familiar surroundings and, most importantly, with their memories. What is good for us is not necessarily what we want.

H The urban housing option may be technically sustainable, but individually unacceptable. There still seems to be a perception among planners that new housing investment can be forced into those areas that planners want to see developed, without proper consideration of where the prospective purchasers want to live. There is a fatal flaw in this premise. Housing developers run businesses. They are not irrevocably committed to building houses and they are not obliged to invest their resources in housing development. Unless there is a reasonable prospect of a profit on the capital at risk in a housing project, they may simply choose to invest in some other activity.

Questions 34–39

*Choose **ONE** phrase A–G from the box to complete each of the following key points. Write the appropriate letters **A–G** in boxes 34–39 on your answer sheet.*

The information in the completed sentences should be an accurate summary of points made by the writer.

You may use any phrase more than once.

Example	*Answer*
There will be more green space available …	**E**

34 Residential density in cities will be increased …

35 There are two types of …

36 There are three types of …

37 Developers are unlikely to build houses …

38 Planners might try to dictate …

39 Many people will not be happy …

A people likely to want to live in high-density accommodation.

B living in higher density accommodation.

C if houses are built smaller.

D where old people should live.

E if residential density in cities is increased.

F where people do not want to live.

G attitude towards city living.

The Writing Test

Throughout Section 2 you will get most benefit by writing your own answers to the questions before you read the sample answers given.

About the Writing Test

The Academic Writing test takes 60 minutes. It consists of two tasks. The suggested time for each task is 20 minutes for Task 1 and 40 minutes for Task 2.

The first task requires you to describe a table, graph, chart or process or procedure. The second task requires a written argument. It carries more marks than Task 1.

To get a good score on the writing you **must** answer both tasks.

It does not matter which section you do first.

Getting the Instructions Right

TASK 1

You should spend about 20 minutes on this task.

EXAMPLE

The table/graph/bar charts below show ...

Write a report for a university lecturer describing the information shown below.

You should write at least 150 words.

There are four key points to these instructions:
- the time – 20 minutes
- the number of words – at least 150
- the text – a report, but not in business report format
- the reader – a university lecturer.

TASK 2

You should spend about 40 minutes on this task.

EXAMPLE

> Present a written argument or case to an educated reader with no specialist knowledge of the following topic.
>
> *[Essay topic]*
>
> You should write at least 250 words.
>   You should use your own ideas, knowledge and experience and support your arguments with examples and relevant evidence.

There are four key points to these instructions:
- the time – 40 minutes
- the number of words – at least 250
- the text – a written argument with examples and evidence from your own knowledge
- the reader – an educated person with only general knowledge of the topic.

Task 1

The IELTS Writing Task 1 is an information transfer task which requires you to write a fairly precise account of some information presented in graphic form, such as a graph, table or some form of a pictorial representation of data.
    In order to complete Task 1 successfully, follow these suggestions.
- Do not spend more than 20 minutes completing the task.
- Spend at least 3–5 minutes planning your answer.
- Read the instructions carefully.
- Analyse the illustration.
- Organise the information.
- Draw a conclusion.
- Check over what you have written.

Describing Graphs

Practice

You should spend about 20 minutes on this task.

The graph below shows the area of land from which grain was harvested. Write a report for a university lecturer describing the information in the graph.

You should write at least 150 words.

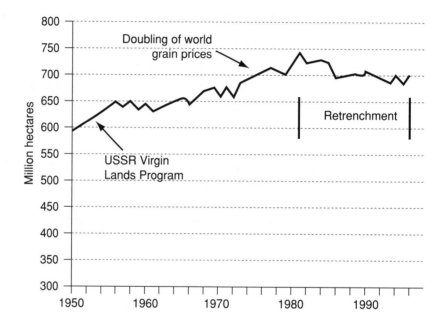

Figure 1   World grain harvested area, 1950–96

Here are some notes written during the planning stage of the essay.

Time/tense	Past time – past tense
Topic	Wld lnd area hvstd 1950–96
General trend	1950–80 ↗, then ↘
	USSR virg lnds prgm ⇨ grt ↗
	Wld prcs 2x ⇨ rpd ↗
	Rtrchmnt ⇨ grad ↘
Conclusion	Grn lnd affctd gov pol & mkt frcs

Explanation

⇨ = cause
↗ = increase
↘ = decrease
2x = doubled/2 times

Notice how words have been abbreviated by leaving out the vowels. This is a useful way of making notes in English. If you do this regularly, you will find that it becomes quite easy to remember what words the abbreviations represent.

EXERCISE 1

Time target – none

This exercise is to give you practice with abbreviations. Here are the abbreviations used in the notes above. Write the full word beside each one.

1 wld		9 rtrchmnt	
2 lnd		10 grad	
3 hvstd		11 grn	
4 virg		12 affctd	
5 prgm		13 gov	
6 grt		14 pol	
7 prcs		15 mkt	
8 rpd		16 frcs	

There are other ways to abbreviate these words. You should develop your own way of abbreviating in English.

When planning your essay it is important to:
- know exactly what is required to complete the task
- brainstorm similar words from the topic so the subjects of your sentences can be written in your own words
- determine the time period so that the correct tense is used
- develop a general statement that gives an overall impression of the graph
- decide which significant details will be discussed to reflect the task requirement
- draw a relevant conclusion or summarise what you have written.

In the exam you can write notes on the illustration and in a clearly defined space on the front of your answer paper. Your notes should be in abbreviated form in order to save time. They should also be organised in the same way as you are going to write the essay.

EXERCISE 2

Time target – 5 minutes

Write a report for a university lecturer describing the information on the graph. You should write at least 150 words.

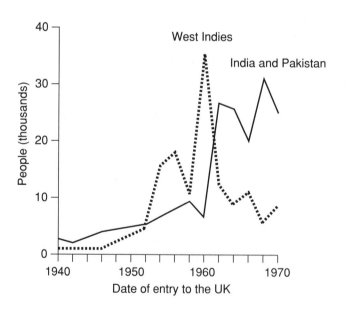

Figure 2

Analyse the graph and fill in the blanks to complete the notes.

These notes will be used later in this chapter to write a full-length Task 1 response.

Time/tense	**(1)** _____
Topic	**(2)** _____ immgrnts frm India & Pak and W Indies to Engld.
General trend	Immgn India & Pak and W Indies **(3)** _____1940–60. Aftr 1960 immgn frm W Indies **(4)** _____. Immgn frm India & Pak **(5)** _____.
Details	India & Pak W Indies 1940–60 **(6)** _____ 1940–60 **(9)** _____ 1960–65 **(7)** _____ 1960–63 **(10)** _____ 1965–70 **(8)** _____ 1963–70 **(11)** _____
Conclusion	# Indian & Pak immgrnts up to present?

Once you have planned your answer you are ready to write it.

Task 1 Essay Plan

- One sentence to introduce the illustration.
- One or two sentences that demonstrate the relationships between the data or show a trend.
- More in-depth description of the data that expands your general statement.
- One sentence to conclude your writing.

Here is an answer to the Practice on page 102.

Introduction

The graph in Figure 1 shows the total world grain harvest area in millions of hectares between 1950 and 1996.

General statement

In general, the total harvest area increased until 1980, at which point there was a reduction in the area harvested due to retrenchment.

Description

In 1950 almost 600 million hectares of grain were harvested world-wide. During the 1950s the USSR initiated a Virgin Lands Program which greatly increased the area harvested to around 650 million hectares. From this point until the mid-1970s the area harvested increased slowly, with some fluctuations, to just over 700 million hectares. Then around 1975 the price of grain doubled and this caused a rapid increase in the amount of land devoted to grain production until 1980. From 1980 to 1995 there was a gradual decrease in the amount of land used for grain cultivation. After this the area harvested again began to rise.

Conclusion/Summary

In summary, we can see that the area devoted to grain production was affected by both government policy and market forces.

[166 words]

Note: *You should not write section headings in your answer to Task 1 in the real IELTS. We have included them here to help you analyse the structure of the essays.*

Language Study

Now we will look at some important language used to describe graphs. Look at the graph in Figure 3.

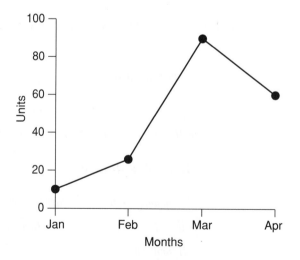

Figure 3   Sales of computers, 1995

Here are some notes to describe the graph.

- 1995 – past tense
- Jan – Feb   increased slightly
- Feb – Mar   increased dramatically
- Mar – Apr   decreased moderately

We can write these notes in complete sentences.

Time period	Subject of the sentence	Verb to describe change	Adverb to describe how much change
From January to February	sales	increased	slightly
From February to March	sales	rose	dramatically
From March to April	sales	fell	moderately

Study the following table.

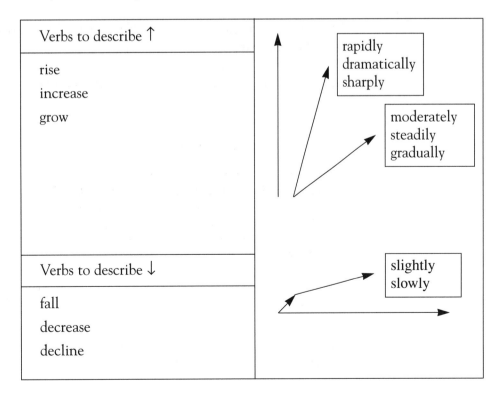

Verbs to describe ↑	
rise	
increase	
grow	

Verbs to describe ↓	
fall	
decrease	
decline	

EXERCISE 3

Time target – 10 minutes

Look at the graphs and write short sentences to describe the information given in each graph. There are sample answers in the Answer Key.

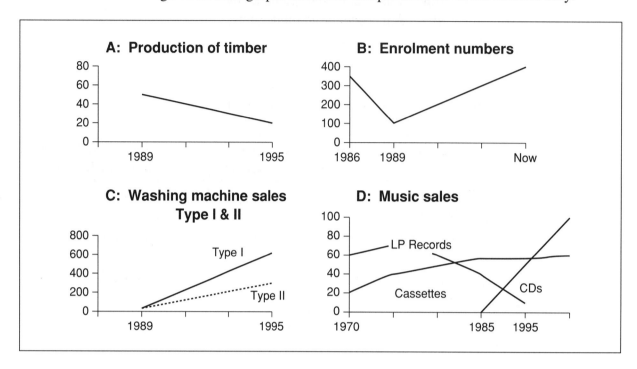

Figure 4

Look at Figure 3 again. In describing the graph, we constructed our sentences the following way.

Subject + **verb** to describe change + **adverb** to describe the amount of change

Sales   *increased*   *slightly*

We could also express the same thing this way.

Time period	'there' to introduce the subject	adjective to describe the amount of change	noun to describe change	
From January to February,	**there** was a	slight	increase	in sales.
From February to March,		dramatic	rise	
From March to April,		moderate	fall	

These sentences mean the same but the grammar has changed. The actions that were expressed with a verb are now expressed with a noun. Therefore adjectives are used instead of adverbs to express the amount of change. Being able to use both forms gives you variety in your sentence structure.

'There' +	article	adjective	noun to describe change	in 'what'
There is		slight	increase	in sales.
was		slow	rise	
has been	a	moderate	growth	
will be		gradual	fall	
		dramatic	drop	
			decrease	
			decline	

EXERCISE 4

Look at the graphs in Exercise 3. Describe each graph again using the noun form.

There are sample sentences in the Answer Key.

Time target – 5 minutes

Describing Trends

Look at the following graph.

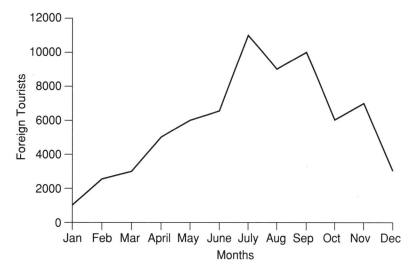

Figure 5 Number of tourists visiting a particular country

We could start at January and describe each month from January to December. However, that would just repeat exactly what the graph shows. It would not demonstrate your understanding and interpretation of what the graph shows.

In this situation we need to describe the trends. Look at the following notes.

- Jan – mid-July # trsts ↗ trnd / peak July
- Jly – Sept # trsts fluctuated
- Sept – Dec # trsts ↘ trnd / slght ↗ Oct

So we could write a description like this.

From January there was an upward trend in the number of tourists and it reached a peak in July. Then, from July to September the number of tourists fluctuated. From September to December there was a downward trend in the number of tourists with a slight rise in October.

Study the graphs and the language in Figures 6 and 7.

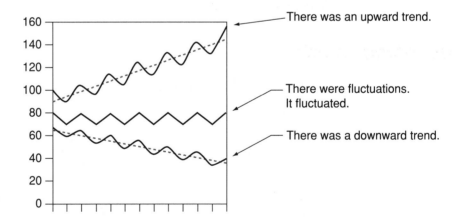

Figure 6

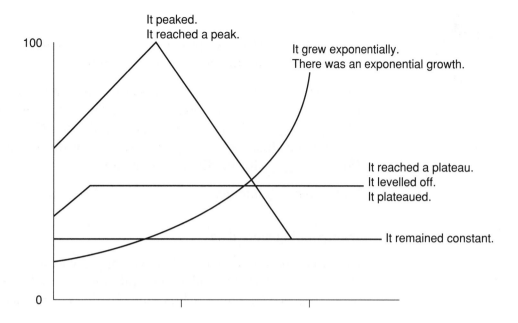

Figure 7

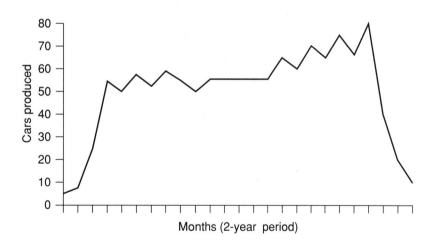

Figure 8   Number of new model cars produced

EXERCISE 5

Look at the graph on car production (Figure 8) and fill in the blanks with a word or a phrase to complete the description.

There was a(n) **(1)** _____ in car production for the first three months. For the next six months the number of cars produced **(2)** _____. Then for five months production **(3)** _____. There was a slight **(4)** _____ over the next seven months before it **(5)** _____ for the final three months.

Time target – 3 minutes

Incorporating more data

Now that you know how to describe change you still need to incorporate more data so that the reader can easily follow the description. Study this description of Figure 8. Note how more data has been included in the description.

> For the first three months car production increased _from_ about five cars per month _to_ just under 60 per month. This was an increase _of_ about 55 cars produced for the period. Over the next six months the number of cars produced fluctuated _at_ around 50 cars per month. For a period of five months production remained _at_ approximately just over 50 cars per month. There was a slight upward trend for the next seven months _to_ a peak of nearly 80 cars produced per month before production decreased rapidly _by_ about 70 cars per month _to_ around 10 cars per month.

Study the prepositions in Figure 9 below.

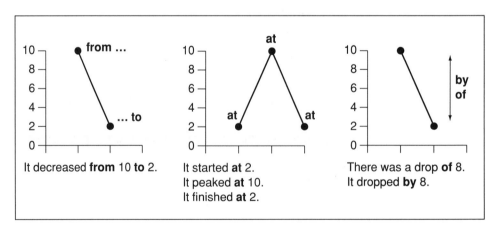

Figure 9

When the graph does not show precise data, use words to express approximation.

Just ⌐ Well ⌐ under	roughly
	nearly
	approximately
Just ⌐ Well ⌐ over	around
	about

EXERCISE 6

Fill in the blanks using the correct preposition. Check your answers in the Answer Key.

Time target – 5 minutes

1 There was an increase _____ just over 50 thousand people.

2 In the first decade the population remained steady _____ approximately 5 million.

3 Unemployment fell _____ just over 500 000 people.

4 Violence in the city peaked _____ about 1500 deaths per 10 000 people.

5 After an initial increase, the city's pollution levels remained constant _____ 5 ppm.

6 The crime rate increased rapidly ____ well over 500 incidents per night.

7 The population is expected to grow exponentially over the next few years and then peak ____ 20 billion people.

8 For the next few months computer prices are expected to drop ____ 50% in spite of a predicted price increase in basic electrical goods ____ 25%.

9 The production of goods is predicted to finish the year ____ 500 units per day.

10 Production began ___ 50 units per day and rose ____ about 20 units per day to end the month ____ well over 600 units.

Sentence subjects

When describing change, it is important to be clear about what is changing. For example, the topic is 'cars'. We cannot say 'cars increased' but 'the number of cars increased', or to avoid repetition, we can say 'car numbers increased'.

Study the language below.

Topic	'The' + measurable quantity + 'of' +topic	Alternatives
Computers	(The) sales of computers	Computer sales
Migrants	The number of migrants	Migrant numbers
Land	The area of land	Land area
Timber	(The) production of timber	Timber production
Crime	(The) level(s) of crime	Crime levels

EXERCISE 7

Time target – 3 minutes

Complete this table.

Topic	'The' + measurable quantity + 'of' +topic	Alternatives
(1) _____	The area of land	(2) _____
(3) _____	(4) _____	Insurance costs
Unemployment	(5) _____	(6) _____
(7) _____	The salaries of females	Female salaries

Time periods

Look at this sentence.

From January to February, there was a slight increase in sales.

We could also say the same thing this way.

Time period	Sentence
For one month, For a period of one month, Over the next month, During the next month,	there was a slight increase in sales

The description of Figure 8 in the section for incorporating data and the description in the Practice on page 112 give more examples of time expressions.

EXERCISE 8

From your notes in Exercise 2 (page 104), complete the following Task 1 exercise. The introduction and conclusion have been written for you.

There is a sample answer in the Answer Key.

Time target – 10 minutes

The graph shows the number of West Indians and Indians and Pakistanis immigrating to the UK from before 1940 to 1970.

As can be seen, immigration of both West Indians and Indians and Pakistanis increased rapidly over a twenty-year period. After 1960 the number of West Indian immigrants decreased rapidly whereas the number of Indian and Pakistani immigrants continued to increase.

Write a detailed description of approximately 90 words. Write on a separate piece of paper.

In conclusion, it is possible to speculate that immigration from India and Pakistan may have continued to increase up to the present day, whereas West Indian immigration may have continued to decrease.

Describing Charts

The approach to writing a description of a chart is similar to writing a description of a graph. Only the language used is different.

Practice

You should spend about 20 minutes on this task.

It is often claimed that women have achieved greater freedom and have access to the same opportunities as men. The pie charts below show some employment patterns in Great Britain.

Write a report for a university lecturer describing the information in the charts below.

You should write at least 150 words.

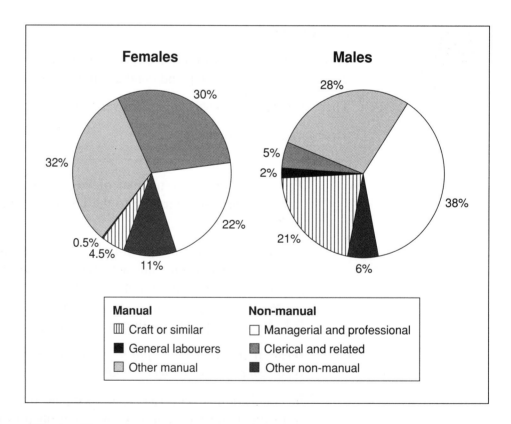

Figure 10

Here are some notes made during the planning stage of the essay.

Time/tense	None given – present simple tense
Topic	Emplymnt % ♀ & ♂
General trend	Mngrl & prof, craft ♀ < ♂, clrcl ♀ > ♂, othr mnl ♀ = ♂
Details	Non-mnl – clrcl ♀, mngrl & prof ♂, other ♀
	Mnl – most crft ♂, gen lab ♂, other ♂ = ♀

Explanation

< = less/fewer than

> = more/greater than

♀ = females/women

♂ = males/men

Here is a sample answer to this Practice for Task 1.

The two pie charts show the proportion of males and females in employment in 6 broad categories, divided into manual and non-manual occupations. In general, a greater percentage of women work in non-manual occupations than work in manual occupations, and the reverse is true for men.

In the non-manual occupations, while a greater percentage of working women than men are found in clerical-type positions, there is a smaller percentage of women than men employed in managerial and professional positions. The percentage of women employed in other non-manual occupations is slightly larger than the percentage of men in these occupations.

In manual employment, the biggest difference between the two sexes is in the employment of craft workers, where males make up 21% of the workforce and females just 4.5%. Furthermore, the percentage of women working as general labourers is very small, only 0.5%. There is not a great deal of difference between the percentage of men doing other forms of manual work (28%) and women in other manual work (32%).

In conclusion, the two charts clearly show that women do not have the same access as men to certain types of employment.

[192 words]

EXERCISE 9

Write notes for Figure 11.

There are sample notes in the Answer Key.

Time target – 5 minutes

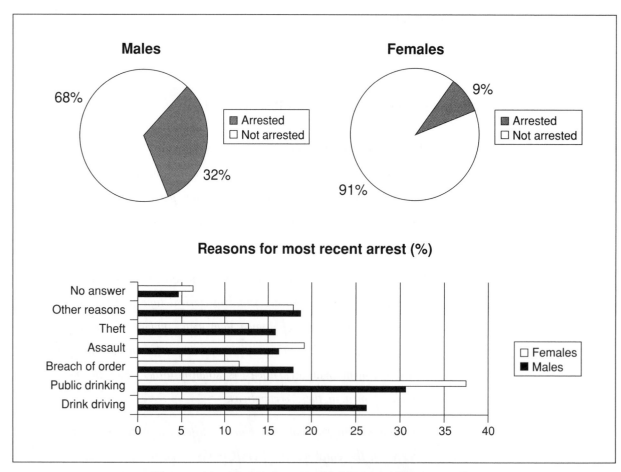

**Figure 11   Persons arrested in past five years –
reasons for most recent arrest, 1994**

Look at this pie chart.

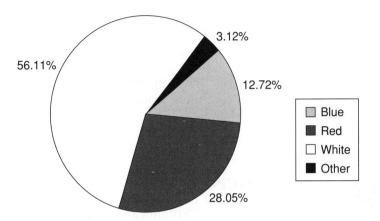

Figure 12   Car colours

When describing charts, the language of comparison is used.

- Describing just one part of the chart

The	most popular second most common	car colour colour	is white. is red.

- Comparing two parts of the pie chart

Red	is	substantially considerably a lot far much somewhat significantly slightly fractionally	more common less popular	than	blue.

- Or

White	is	about twice three times	as	common popular	as	red.

Note: We cannot say, 'The least popular colour is other'. 'Other' is not a colour but means all the other colours not mentioned here.

We can also interpret the chart and say, 'People **buy** more white cars than red cars'.

But be careful. It is better not to say, 'People **prefer buying** white cars to blue cars'.

We cannot tell from the chart whether buyers have a restricted range of colours to choose from. Buyers may choose a colour based on availability rather than preference.

EXERCISE 10

Time target – 5 minutes for each chart

Look at the following charts in Figures 13 and 14 and write a simple description of each.

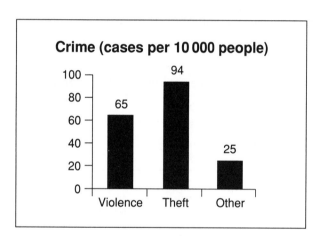

Figure 13

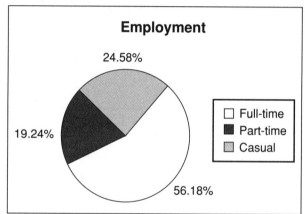

Figure 14

Look at Figure 12 and study these examples.

White, **which is 56.11%**, is considerably more common than blue, **which makes up 12.72%**.

Red, **which constitutes 28.05%**, is about twice as popular as blue, **which is 12.72%**.

The other colours, **which constitute 3.12%**, are considerably less popular than blue **(12.72%)**.

There are two ways of incorporating data: by using
- brackets (   )
- a relative clause (**which** + appropriate verb: is, makes up, constitutes, accounts for).

EXERCISE 11

Look at the charts in Figures 13 and 14 and rewrite your sentences to include data.

Time target – 3 minutes per chart

Writing introductory sentences

Look at these examples.

> The graph in Figure 1 shows the total grain harvest area in millions of hectares between 1950 and 1996.

> The two pie charts show the proportion of males and females in employment in 6 broad categories.

To write an introductory sentence, use your own words. If you copy the title of an illustration or the question word for word, the examiner will regard this as plagiarism and ignore the sentence. This could affect your Task 1 band score.

	Type of chart	Appropriate verb	Description
The	illustration graph pie chart bar chart table	shows illustrates presents	the number of … the proportion of … information on … data on …

To avoid plagiarism, change the words.

Example

> The two pie charts show the proportion of males and females in employment in 6 broad categories

↓

> The two pie charts give the proportion of men and women employed in 6 broad areas

Or, change the structure.

Example

> The two pie charts show the proportion of males and females in employment in 6 broad categories.

↓

> The two pie charts show, in 6 broad categories, the proportion of males and females in employment.

You could change the way you express the time period.

Example

The graph in Figure 1 shows the total grain harvest area in millions of hectares between 1950 and 1996.

The graph in Figure 1 shows the total grain harvest area in millions of hectares over a 36-year period.

EXERCISE 12

Look at Figure 11 and write a simple introductory sentence. Then, using your notes, write a full answer to the task. Write on a separate piece of paper.

Time target – 20 minutes

> **Review**
>
> In this section you have learnt how to:
> ✔ describe charts by using the language of comparison
> ✔ incorporate statistical data
> ✔ write sentences to introduce the illustration.

Describing Tables

Describing tables is similar to describing charts. The same structures of comparison and contrast are used. The most challenging aspect is dealing with considerable amounts of data.

When describing tables:
- do not describe all the data presented
- look for significant data; e.g. the highest, the lowest, etc.
- try and group the data. This may require you to use some general knowledge of the world, such as recognising developed and developing countries.

Practice

You should spend about 20 minutes on this task.

The following table gives statistics showing the aspects of quality of life in five countries.

Write a report for a university lecturer describing the information in the table below.

You should write at least 150 words.

Country	GNP per head (1982: US dollars)	Daily calorie supply per head	Life expectancy at birth (years)	Infant mortality rates (per 1000 live births)
Bangladesh	140	1877	40	132
Bolivia	570	2086	50	124
Egypt	690	2950	56	97
Indonesia	580	2296	49	87
USA	13 160	3652	74	12

Figure 15 Selected statistics showing aspects of the quality of life in 5 countries

Here are some notes made during the planning stage.

Time/tense	1982 – past t
Topic	stnd livg 5 cntrys
General comment	USA (Indstrl) > Other Count (Devg)
Details	Qual of L: Egy = Indo = Bol
	Egy highest, Bang lowest
	But Indo IMR < Egy
	Bang: USA
	GNP: 1/100
	Cal & Life exp: $\frac{1}{2}$
	IMR 10 ✖
Conclusion	Oth count must devel lot more = USA

Explanation

> = greater than

< = less than

IMR = infant mortality rate

Here is a sample answer.

The table uses four broad economic indicators to show the standard of living in five selected countries in 1982.

As can be seen, the USA — an industrialised country — had the highest GNP and daily calorie intake, the longest life expectancy and the lowest infant mortality rate. The other developing countries had a considerably lower quality of life.

Egypt, Indonesia and Bolivia were similar in their range of indicators, with Egypt having the highest quality of life amongst the three. However, Egypt's infant mortality rate was slightly higher than Indonesia's, at 97 deaths per 1000 compared to 87 in Indonesia.

Bangladesh had by far the lowest quality of life in all the four indicators. Its GNP was one hundred times smaller than the USA's. Its calorie intake and life expectancy were about half those in the USA and its infant mortality rate was 10 times greater.

In conclusion, it can be seen from the economic indicators that the four developing countries have to develop a lot more before reaching the same level of quality of life as the USA.

[178 words]

EXERCISE 13

Time target – 5 minutes

The following table shows the average incomes of scientists employed by the National Institute of Health (NIH).

Write notes for this table. Alternatively, you can circle, underline or highlight points you would group together when writing your response. Remember, you can write on the question paper. There is no Answer Key for this exercise.

Position	Male (number)	Female (number)	Difference
Total MD	$89 219 (483)	$ 85 274 (71)	–$ 3 945
Total PhD	$74 024 (473)	$ 64 903 (118)	–$ 9 121
Lab chief MD	$95 185 (138)	$105 696 (7)	+$10 509
Lab Chief PhD	$89 827 (78)	$ 89 484 (2)	–$ 197
Section Chief MD	$89 653 (157)	$ 86 022 (21)	–$ 3 631
Section Chief PhD	$76 819 (140)	$ 73 570 (31)	–$ 3 247
Investigator MD	$83 249 (177)	$ 81 585 (43)	–$ 1 664
Investigator PhD	$67 131 (251)	$ 61 164 (85)	–$ 5 972
Staff fellow PhD	$34 642 (14)	$ 31 888 (9)	–$ 2 794

Figure 16   Pay of NIH scientists by gender

Grouping Data

EXERCISE 14

Time target – 5 minutes

Look at the following table and determine:

a how you would group the data
b what significant data points you would describe.

Sport	Number of Students	Hours spent per month
Rugby	150	20
Swimming	56	35
Football	180	15
Cricket	109	20
Athletics	45	40
Golf	25	35
Baseball	110	23
Tennis	56	30

Figure 17

To signal your conclusion you can use the terms in the box.

Expression	What to write
In summary, … To sum up, …	Express the main point of the illustration again in your own words.
In conclusion, … To conclude, …	Say something new that does not extend too far beyond what the illustration shows. You can mention future implications, or draw a conclusion as in the sample answer to Exercise 12.

Look at these examples.

Example 1 refers to Figure 1 in the Practice section on page 102.

In summary, we can see that the area devoted to grain production was affected by both government policy and market forces.

As the graph has no distinct overall trend, we cannot predict what 'may happen in the future'.

Here we need some knowledge of the real world to realise that the USSR Virgin Lands Program was a government policy and retrenchment and doubling of World Grain prices were related to market forces.

Example 2 refers to Figure 10 in Practice 7.

In conclusion, the two charts clearly show that women do not have the same access as men to certain positions of employment.

This conclusion is a response to the opening statement that 'women … have access to the same opportunities as men'.

Example 3 refers to Figure 15 in Practice 8.

In conclusion, it can be seen that from the economic indicators, the four developing countries have to develop a lot more before reaching the same level of quality of life as the USA.

Here you have to have some knowledge of the fact that there is one developed country and three developing countries represented in the table. This conclusion summarises the information by stating the obvious disparity between the developed and developing countries.

EXERCISE 15

Time target – 15 minutes

Here are the complete instructions for Figure 16 in Exercise 13. Write a full response to the task. Write on a separate piece of paper.

You should spend about 20 minutes on this task.

The table below shows the average incomes of scientists employed by the National Institute of Health (NIH).

Write a report for a university lecturer describing the information in the table below.

You should write at least 150 words.

Process Description

These questions rarely appear on the IELTS Test. They are different to other types of questions because:
• the language is different
• they test your ability to describe, expand and link each important stage in the illustration.

Practice

You should spend about 20 minutes on this task.

Scientists and engineers are continuing to look for new ways to generate electricity. The following is a diagram of how electricity may be generated from tidal flow.

Write a report for a university lecturer that describes the diagram.

You should write at least 150 words

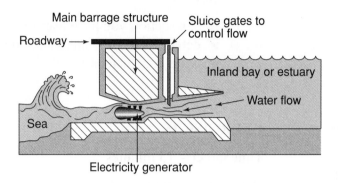

Main barrage structure

Sluice gates to
control flow

Roadway →

Inland bay or estuary

Water flow

Sea

Electricity generator

Figure 18

This is how the essay might be planned

Topic	Elcty gentd fr H_2O pow
Stages	Main const + rd
	Sluice gate open
	H_2O fr incmg tide pass genr
	Elcty gentd
Conclusion	clean + prptl enrgy, – effic ∵ time tid chgs

Here is a sample answer to the question.

The diagram shows how electricity can be generated from rising and falling tides.

A structure which houses turbines is built across a bay or somewhere where a large body of water can be contained. The structure can also have a roadway built on top of it, thus providing dual services. When the water level on one side of the structure is significantly higher than the other side, i.e. at high tide or at low tide, the sluice gates are opened to allow the water to flow. The water passes through tunnels where the generators are housed and causes them to spin. This creates electricity, which is then harnessed for use.

In conclusion, although this method is a clean and perpetual source of energy, it appears to be rather inefficient as it is dependent on the tidal changes, which have a rather slow cycle.

[143 words]

Language Study

Describing how something works often requires us to use the passive voice in the present tense.

The present simple passive			
Subject	**is/are**	**past participle**	**(by agent)**
The handle	*is*	*turned*	*by the operator.*

Analysis

Read the following short paragraph on how rice is grown and determine why some sentences are in the passive and some are in the active. Analyse how the stages are linked together.

First, The paddy-field is prepared and flooded. Then, the rice seeds are planted in a small area of the field. The seedlings grow for about 6 weeks and then are transplanted to the main field. The plants mature and after about 5 months the rice is finally harvested.

EXERCISE 16

Time target – 20 minutes

A lot of administrative work is done after the IELTS Test. Below is a chart of what happens to the candidate's IELTS Test after the test has been completed.

Describe the chart.

You should write at least 150 words.

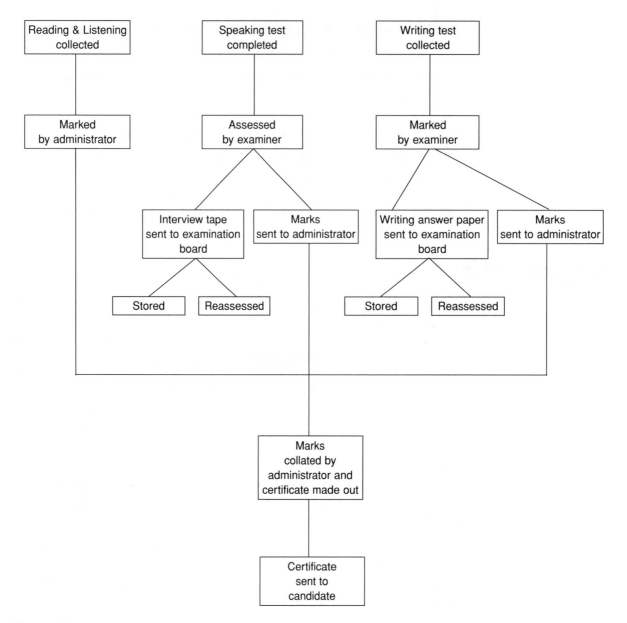

Figure 19

How Task I is Assessed

The examiner reads your answer and awards a band score of between 1 (did not answer the question) and 9 (native speaker-like) under three categories.

- Task fulfilment (TF)

  The examiner determines whether you answered the question or not.

- Coherence and cohesion (CC)

  The examiner determines whether you have written an essay that is easily understood and is well organised.

- Vocabulary and sentence structure (VSS)

  The examiner determines whether your vocabulary is appropriate and your sentence structure has variety and accuracy.

The band scores are then added together, divided by 3 and rounded to determine your band score for this task.

For example:　　TF　　　　= 　5
　　　　　　　　CC　　　　= 　6
　　　　　　　　VSS　　　 = 　6
　　　　　　　　Overall band = 　6

Discussion of Sample Essays

Sample 1

The graphs below show information on the production of consumer goods and the consumption of television sets in Russia.

Write a report for a university lecturer describing the information in the graphs below.

You should write at least 150 words.

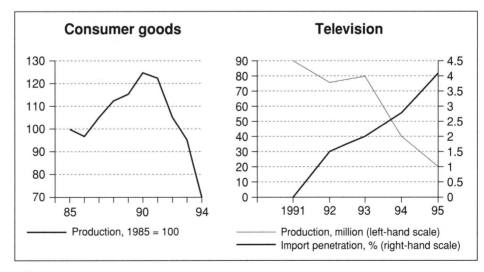

Figure 20

This how a student might have answered this task.

The graphs present information on the number of TV sets imported and bought and the overall production of consumer goods in Russia in the last decade.

The production of consumer goods in 1985 stood at 100 million. Then there was a slight decrease and then a steady rise to reach approximately 125 million goods in 1990. After this peak the production fell sharply to 70 million goods in 1994.

The production of TV sets in 1991 was approximately 90 million. Then television production fell steadily, except for a slight rise in 1993, to around 20 million TV sets in 1995. The percentage of TV sets increased from 0% to just over 4% in 1995. This was a steady rise.

In conclusion, the drop in consumer goods was due to the economic difficulties in Russia.

[134 words]

COMMENT

This essay is reasonably successful because:
- the details are nearly complete (the comments made on each graph line are brief and reasonably accurate)
- it is well organised
- the sentences are also easy to understand
- the sentences are varied and accurate.

However, it didn't quite answer the task. Although the details are complete, there is no general statement to mention how the graphs related to each other, i.e. 'Consumer production decreased which affected TV production. In contrast, there was an increase in the number of imported TV sets.'

Also, the conclusion is inaccurate. The language used is too definite. There may have been other causes of the changes in the graph, i.e. 'The drop in consumer production was possibly due to…'

You should spend about 20 minutes on this task.

Many women want or need to continue working even after they have children. The charts below show the working patterns of mothers with young children to care for.

Write a report for a university lecturer describing the information in the charts below.

You should write at least 150 words.

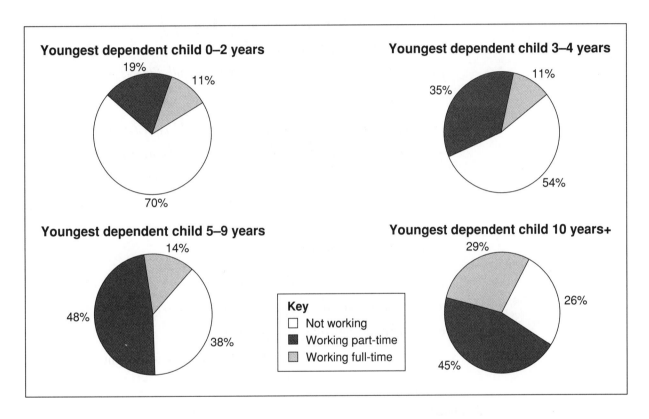

Figure 21 Working patterns of mothers with young children, Great Britain

Here is how a student might have answered this task.

In Great Britain, there are many women who want or need to continue working even after they have children. The four charts show the working patterns of mothers with young children to care for.

At first, mothers with their youngest dependent child aged 0–2 years, there is 11% women working full-time and 19% women working part time. The women who are not working is 70%.

The mothers with youngest dependent child aged between 3 to 4 years, almost half of them not work. There is 46% women working part time and the women who are working full time is 11%. It increase.

Then, the mothers with youngest dependent child aged between 5–9 years 38% of them are not working. There is 48% women working part time and the women who are working full time is 14%. The number of women working full time was increase in this chart and the number of working part time increase 13% from chart 2 and increase 29% from chart 1.

Finally, the chart 4 showed that the mother with dependent child aged 10 years has the biggest percentage number. There is 45% women working full time and 25% part time.

[162 words. Note: The first 2 sentences were ignored.]

COMMENT

This essay has a few problems because:
- the sentences are not varied and there are some grammatical errors (Each paragraph is basically expressed the same way.)
- it is not very well organised (The overall structure of the essay is good. However, the details within each paragraph are not consistent: e.g. 'from largest percentage to smallest percentage' or 'from women not working to women working full time'.)
- some of it is not very easy to understand (The writer tried to mention the changes from chart to chart. It would have been easier to do this as a general statement.)

However, the writer has tried to answer the question and most details were reported.

You should spend about 20 minutes on this task.

Housing is a basic human need and is important to the economy of a country. Below is a table of a survey on types of housing in Australia.

Describe the information in the table.

You should write at least 150 words.

	Separate house	**Semi-detached/ row or terrace house/ town house**	**Flat/unit/ apartment**	**Other**	**Total**
New South Wales	1705.3 (76%)	183.4 (8%)	343.9 (16%)	4.6	2237.2
Victoria	1344.8 (81%)	98.8 (6%)	212.7 (13%)	1.3	1657.6
Queensland	985.0 (82%)	54.9 (5%)	150.7 (13%)	3.4	1194.1
South Australia	457.0 (78%)	93.0 (16%)	35.4 (6%)	2.5	587.9
Western Australia	521.3 (82%)	71.1 (11%)	45.1 (7%)	3.1	640.7
Tasmania	155.3 (85%)	9.7 (5%)	17.7 (10%)	0.5	183.3
Northern Territory	42.0 (63%)	6.4 (10%)	16.6 (25%)	1.4	66.5
Australian Capital Territory	89.9 (82%)	10.4 (9%)	10.3 (9%)	–	110.6
Australia	**5300.7 (79%)**	**527.9 (8%)**	**832.5 (12%)**	**16.8**	**6677.9**

Figure 22 Number of dwellings by State/Territory, 1994 ('000)

Here is how a student might have answered the task.

Housing satisfies the essential human needs for shelter, security and privacy. Internationally, shelter is recognised as a basic human right. The adequacy or otherwise of housing is therefore an important component of individual wellbeing. Housing also has an enormous significance in the national economy, with its influence on investment levels, interest rates, building activity and employment.

The table shows that the separate house was the most popular type of dwelling in Australia in 1994, which made up 79% of all dwellings. Tasmania had the highest proportion of separate houses (85%) and the northern territory the lowest (63%). All other States and the Australian Capital Territory were in the range of 76 to 82%.

Flats or apartments were in the next most common type of dwellings. Twelve per cent of dwellings in Australia were of this design. South Australia (6%) and Western Australia (7%) had relatively low percentages of flats or apartments. The Northern Territory with 25% had the highest proportion of flats or apartments.

[160 words]

COMMENT

This essay has some problems because:
- some of it did not answer the question (The introduction is too long and irrelevant.)
- some important details are missing (One column of the table was not mentioned.)

However, it is well organised and easy to understand, and the sentences are accurate and varied.

Task 2

Writing Task 2 is different from Task 1 because:
- you are writing for an educated non-specialist audience and not a university lecturer. Therefore your language need not be as formal
- you are expected to give your opinion
- you have to write 250 words in 40 minutes instead of 150 in 20 minutes.

Before writing your answer you should spend five minutes planning. These are steps that you should go through.
- Read the questions and the instructions carefully.
- Analyse the topic and the focus.
- Decide what you think about the question.
- Brainstorm ideas to be used in your answer.
- Fit these ideas into an essay plan divided into paragraphs.
- Begin writing your introduction.

Topic/Focus

> Present a written argument or case to an educated non-specialist audience on the following statement.
>
> *The internet will bring about a new freedom of information and so narrow the technology gap between developed and developing countries.*

In the question above the topic is the internet. We know this because the internet is the subject of the sentence. However this does not mean that the examiner wants you to write down everything you know about the internet.

The rest of the sentence focuses the topic to the internet's effect on the freedom of information and on the possibility of it narrowing the technology gap. The question asks you to 'write an argument or case' which means that you must argue for or against the statement.

Therefore the question is:

> *Will the internet bring about a new freedom of information and will this freedom of information narrow the technology gap?*

Another way of analysing a question is to underline key words, as in the question below.

> *Due to the <u>increase in unemployment</u> in many countries, <u>companies</u> are beginning <u>to retire</u> their <u>employees early</u>. This leads to a <u>loss of valuable expertise</u>. <u>At what age do you think people should retire?</u>*

The topic of this essay is the actual question: At what age should people retire? The focus is: Companies lose valuable expertise by retiring employees early.

EXERCISE 17

Time target – 5 minutes

Look at the sample Task 2 questions below and write down the actual question you are being asked.

1 *As public safety is of the highest importance, it is often necessary to test new products on animals. It is better for a few animals to suffer than for human life to be placed at risk by untested products.*

Write a report for an educated non-specialist audience for or against the above.

2 *If countries are serious about solving traffic problems, they should tax private cars very heavily and use the money to provide free or very cheap rail travel.*

To what extent do you agree with the above?

3 *The quality of health care a person receives should not depend on the size of their bank balance. The government is responsible for providing a high level of health care for all its citizens.*

To what extent do you agree or disagree with the above statement?

EXERCISE 18

Look at the three Task 2 questions below. The topic is the same. How is the focus different?

1 *Women should give up their jobs and go back to their traditional role of home-maker in order to reduce world unemployment.*

Write a report for an educated non-specialist audience for or against the above.

2 *One solution to the decline in moral values in today's world would be for men and women to return to their traditional roles.*

Write a report for an educated non-specialist audience for or against the above.

3 *Women will play an increasingly important role in the workplace of the future.*

To what extent do you agree with the above?

Brainstorming

> Present a written argument or case to an educated non-specialist audience on the following statement.
>
> *The internet will bring about a new freedom of information and so narrow the technology gap between developed and developing countries.*

Brainstorming is when you think of as many ideas on a subject as possible. For example, for the question above, you might come up with ideas like these.

- World-wide communication possible.
- Greater access to information.
- Only the rich can afford access to the internet.
- Computing skills are necessary to operate the internet so new technology gap developing.
- Makes the copyright laws hard to enforce so difficult to keep technology secret.
- Difficult to censor.

After you have thought of as many ideas as possible you should organise them. One way of organising your ideas is to divide them into ideas for and against the statement.

EXERCISE 19

Time target – 3 minutes

Put the ideas above into the table divided into 'for' and 'against'.

For	Against

EXERCISE 20

Look at the sample questions in Exercise 17 and brainstorm and organise ideas for at least one of them.

Now link your ideas together to form paragraphs.

Time target – 5 minutes per question

The Answer Key has suggestions for the brainstorming only. You should get someone (your teacher or someone who has good English) to comment on and evaluate your paragraphs.

Writing the Essay — The Introduction

In many ways, your conclusion and introduction are very similar in that they both state *your opinion*. The introduction is probably the shortest section of a Task 2 essay. *It might contain:*
- a restatement of the question
- your opinion
- what and how you are going to discuss the question.

When you write your introduction do not:
- copy the question word for word
- give a lot of background information.

PRACTICE

Look at the following three introductions to the question below and decide which you like better and why.

> *If countries are serious about solving traffic problems, they should tax private cars very heavily and use the money to provide free or very cheap rail travel.*
>
> To what extent do you agree with the above?

Introduction 1

Many nations are facing massive traffic congestion in their cities. This both makes travel difficult and causes environmental damage. In order to solve this problem it is necessary to establish alternative transportation systems such as railways. In my opinion the best way to finance the development of public transport is to tax car drivers.

Introduction 2

Motor cars were invented at the end of the last century and have developed greatly over the last 100 years. In many countries families have two cars and sometimes even three. As there are so many cars on the road there are often traffic jams on major roads. It can take many hours to complete a short journey at peak times in some major cities. Many attempts have been made to solve the problems of bad traffic. These include limiting the times cars are allowed to drive in certain areas and making cars carry a certain number of passengers. These schemes have met with varying degrees of success.

Introduction 3

Many people say that if countries are serious about solving traffic problems, they should tax private cars very heavily and use the money to provide free rail travel.

An explanation

Introduction 1 is good as it restates the question in different words and states the candidate's position on the subject.

Introduction 2 gives irrelevant background information (e.g. when cars were invented, how many cars people have).

Introduction 3 is too close to the original statement in the question.

EXERCISE 21

Write an introduction for this Task 2 question.

> *A country's first duty to its citizens is to protect them. Therefore it is logical that defence should take up a significant proportion of the national budget.*
>
> Write a report for an educated non-specialist audience for or against the above.

Remember to analyse the topic and the focus of the question before you start. You might also find it useful to brainstorm the ideas you want to include before beginning to write.

Time target – 3 minutes

The Argument

Although you may have strong opinions about a topic or a question, you should also state the opposing arguments to your case, to show that you understand both sides of the problem.

PRACTICE

Look at a section of the writer's plan and final paragraphs for the question below to see how this was done.

> *Too much education is dangerous. If people receive more education than they need to function in their job, it only breeds dissatisfaction.*
>
> Write a report for an educated non-specialist audience for or against the above.

Plan

For	Against
Gives people unreal expectations	How do you decide the level of education a person needs?
Expensive	High level human resources necessary for development
Not enough challenging jobs to meet people's expectations	Uneducated people unable to show initiative
Students a major cause of disruption, reject authority	People have the right to attain self-fulfilment

Extract from essay

Some people may say that education gives people unrealistic ambitions; the law of the market place decrees that not every one can be a managing director. In fact for every boss there must be many more employees, so some countries believe there is very little point in training people for a level of job that they can never hope to achieve. What is more, education is expensive. Therefore over-education is a waste of time and money. Another argument against education would be that students tend to be a disruptive influence on society. Once you encourage people to think for themselves it is difficult to control what they are thinking. It is hardly surprising that students are often found at the forefront of radical organisations.

In spite of the problems of over-education, most countries need a high standard of human resources in to order to compete in the world market. Constantly changing technology means that the workforce has to be flexible and receptive to new ideas in order to be of value to employers. When a person is only trained to perform one job, it is not realistic to expect him or her to adapt to a change in circumstances or an unexpected problem. All this is not to mention the moral questions involved in limiting education. Who has the right to say how much education a person is entitled to? What criteria could be used to decide a level of schooling?

It may be true that a greater level of education tends to make people more radical. However, if society is not going to become *static, it must be prepared to accept new ideas. Therefore the degree of radicalism caused by a high level of education can only serve to make the country more adaptable and better able to withstand social change in the long run.*

Think about the following questions. (The answers are immediately below them.)

1   Which paragraph agrees with the statement?

2   Which paragraph disagrees with the statement?

3   How does the writer state her/his opinion?

Answers

1   Paragraph 2

2   Paragraph 1

3   The last sentence expresses the writer's opinion.

EXERCISE 22

Look at the following topics and write two short paragraphs (about 50 words): one supporting the statement and the other against it.

1   Nobody should marry before the age of 30.

2   Everybody has the right to carry a gun.

3   Patriotism is the biggest cause of war.

Time target – 10 minutes for each topic

The Conclusion

A good conclusion summarises the ideas presented in the text and restates the writer's opinion.

EXERCISE 23

Time target – 3 minutes

Look at the notes that a student wrote for this Task 2 question and write a conclusion.

> *If countries are serious about solving traffic problems, they should tax private cars very heavily and use the money to provide free or very cheap rail travel.*

Introduction

Many nations are facing massive traffic congestion in their cities. This both makes travel difficult and causes environmental damage. In order to solve this problem it is necessary to establish alternative transportation systems such as railways.

For	Against
Encourage people to use public transport	Not door-to-door service like cars
Reduce the number of cars on the road	People like owning cars
Cut down on traffic jams/pollution	Increased taxes are always unpopular
Save fossil fuels	Cheap railways would lose money and need state subsidies
More money to develop infrastructure	

Organising the Paragraph

In essays, paragraphs usually have a standard format.
* The *first sentence* is a topic sentence which explains the main point.
* The *next few sentences* develop the theme of the topic sentence.
* The *last sentence* should lead into the next paragraph.

Therefore, a standard paragraph should look like this.

Topic sentence

It is often said that people need to work to feel useful. This is not true.

Supporting arguments

It is doubtful whether most of the jobs people do are of any value to society. It is hard to imagine people getting much satisfaction from the usual paper shuffling that takes place in most offices. Therefore if a lot of jobs are of little value to the world and some jobs are actually harmful to mankind, there is no reason for people to feel guilty about staying at home and doing something more interesting instead. In fact it could be said that in these times of high unemployment it is more useful not to work as you are giving other people opportunities to feel fulfilled.

Summary

As most jobs are neither interesting nor productive, the idea of working to contribute to society is not realistic.

EXERCISE 24

Time target – 5 minutes

Read the following paragraphs and decide on suitable topic sentences.

1 _____

Firstly, every time I go to Capunk it always rains so you can't see anything and if you want to go anywhere you are going to get very wet. Secondly, it is usually very crowded. If you go for a quiet walk, you find yourself bumping into day-trippers eating uninteresting packed lunches from cardboard boxes, while listening to Michael Jackson on their car stereo. Finally, after about 6.00 a.m. traffic is at a total standstill and the cool damp air mixes noxiously with the exhausts of a thousand vehicles. Overall, I think there are better places to go for the weekend.

2 _____

In order to do this it is important for the leaders to earn the trust of their subordinates. Employees need to feel that in a crisis the management will look after their interests and that they will never be asked to do anything that the manager wouldn't be prepared to do him- or herself. This type of relationship can only be established if good channels of communication exist. Therefore motivation is based upon a mixture of mutual trust and good communications.

3 _____

Unfortunately, many developed countries consider it uneconomical to send their food surplus to regions where hunger exists. Also some of the richest nations consider control of the food supply a means of putting pressure on developing countries to make them politically subservient. Another problem is that often the food that is sent to countries suffering from famine does not reach the people who need it. Bureaucracy and corruption cause the food to be stored or sold on the open market.

EXERCISE 25

Write the paragraphs for the following topic sentences. Write on a separate piece of paper.

Time target – 15 minutes

1 Watching too much television reduces people's capacity to think for themselves.

These words and ideas might help you.

Accept opinions/without thinking	Most TV non-educational
Simplistic view of life	Second-hand experience

2 If people are allowed to carry guns the number of murders will increase.

Cohesion

In a good essay, each sentence should be linked logically to the sentence before and the sentence after. Two common ways of doing this are:
- cause and effect
- contrast.

CAUSE AND EFFECT

Example

I went to a party last night | so / . Therefore | I'm tired this morning.

The first sentence is the reason for the second sentence. If we use 'so' we join the two sentences together. If we use 'therefore' we start a new sentence.

It is also possible to change the two sentences round so the first sentence is the result and the second sentence is the reason.

I'm tired this morning | because / as | I went to a party last night.

EXERCISE 26

Time target – 5 minutes

Write the next sentence using reasons or results as necessary. (Some of these sentences can be used as either a reason or a result.) Write them on a separate piece of paper.

1   She found lipstick on his shirt …

2   He woke up …

3   I came to the lesson late …

4   Rainforests are important for the environment …

5   Unleaded petrol reduces exhaust emissions …

6   Most people in prison come from poor social backgrounds …

CONTRAST

Example

The food tasted wonderful | but
. However, | I was sick for three days afterwards.

or

Although the food tasted wonderful, I was sick for three days afterwards.

Often one sentence is used to modify another (add extra and contrasting information to the first sentence). To do this we can use:

- **although**   which usually goes in front of the first sentence. A comma divides the first sentence from the second sentence
- **but**   which usually goes in the middle of the two sentences and requires no extra punctuation
- **however**   which usually begins a new sentence and is followed by a comma.

Remember: You cannot use 'although' and 'but' in the same sentence.
You cannot use 'however' and 'but' in the same sentence.
You cannot use 'although' and 'however' in the same sentence.

EXERCISE 27

Time target – 2 minutes for each group of sentences

Link the sentences in each group together into a paragraph using connecting words.

1   Most countries have made some efforts to control the traffic in their major cities.

   These efforts have often failed.

   The number of cars increases so rapidly that the measures taken are immediately out of date.

2   Floods are a major problem in the city.

   The government seem to be making very little effort to improve the situation.

   They often make speeches about the importance of water catchment areas.

   They continue to build on every available green space.

3   Many people say the space program is a waste of money.

   Developing another planet could be the answer to overpopulation.

   Life may be possible on another planet.

   Life would probably not be very pleasant.

4   Rainforests are a valuable source of biodiversity and new drugs

   They could also be used to feed the poor and provide them with farmland.

   Trees are useful for stopping erosion.

   Logging companies provide jobs and wood product exports are a valuable source of foreign exchange.

Grammar — Tense Check

The Present Simple Tense

The present simple tense is used to describe:
- habits
- things that are always true.

This tense is often used for IELTS Task 2 essays to describe existing situations.

Examples
Many trees take twenty or thirty years to reach their full size.
Many people still don't have enough to eat.
Many governments consider money to be more valuable than people.
The space program is very expensive.

The Present Perfect Tense

The present perfect tense is used in three situations.

1   Events starting in the past and continuing into the present.
Examples
The world population has grown rapidly over the last 100 years.
There have always been wars.
Nuclear weapons have not been used in the last 50 years.

2   Something that happened in the past but has a general present result.
Examples
Mary has had her baby.
Recently prices have risen.
The World Bank has just issued a report.

In all these examples the event happened in the recent past and is still news now.

3   Experience. The present perfect is used to talk about an event that happened in the past, where the time or the frequency are unknown.
Examples
I have seen a ghost. (When?)
Man has been to the moon. (When? How many times?)

In this use of the present perfect, it is not possible to use the continuous form.

For the purposes of Task 2 essays, you are most likely to use 'will' to write about the future.

Examples

The rainforests will vanish in the next 20 years.

Most diseases will be curable in 50 years time.

Remember: 'will' is always followed by a verb in the infinitive without 'to'.

EXERCISE 28

The following IELTS Task 2 essay has 10 mistakes in it. Read the essay and correct the mistakes.

Time target – 10 minutes

> *As most foreign aid often benefits the donor more than the receiver, developing countries should refuse to repay their debts.*
>
> To what extent do you agree?

Over the past 30 years, many countries have spent most of their income repaying the interest on foreign debts. Many people are consider the initial loans, responsible for these debts, to be more beneficial to the lender than to the borrower.

In the past, most developing countries were short of ready funds to build the infrastructure necessary for development. Therefore, foreign countries were asked to provide loans for projects to help the countries will become self reliant. However, this money often to be used to make quick profits for developers or to line the pockets of corrupt officials. Once the money is used the problem of repayment had began.

Since the 1970s many developing countries have found that they can't pay back the loans or even the interest is accumulate on the loans. Consequently the countries have borrowed more money to pay back the interest. This gave western countries the power dictates government policy through the World Bank and the International Monetary Fund. These financial institutions only interest in balance sheets. Therefore nations forced to adopt policies which do nothing to develop their resources or improve the lives of the local people.

Countries that get caught in this debt spiral, had no chance of paying back the initial money borrowed, while the banks making the loans make two or three times the money lent after the interest payments are taken into account. As most donor countries were already repaid both in terms of money and in terms of economic interest, it is morally right for developing countries to refuse to pay back foreign loans.

Future Possibilities

Often in Task 2 essays, it is necessary to speculate on the possible results of a future action. This is often done by using a conditional clause.

Example
   If the rainforests are cut down, they will become deserts.

The first part of the sentence ('If the rain forests are cut down') presents a possible future situation. The second part of the sentence ('they will become deserts') describes the possible future consequences of the first statement.

EXERCISE 29

Write possible consequences for the following situations.

Time target – 10 minutes

1   If the world population continues to increase, …

2   If the number of cars isn't controlled, …

3   If it rains this afternoon, …

4   If I get a band eight in the IELTS Test, …

5   If there is life on another planet, …

The second conditional is also used to speculate about the results of future events. However, the second conditional is used when the events are impossible or the writer considers the events to be very unlikely.

Example
   If aliens landed on earth, they would think human beings were very primitive.

Notice the first part of the sentence uses the past tense while the second section uses 'would' instead of 'will'. Like all modal verbs, 'would' is followed by a verb in the infinitive without 'to'.

Example
   If I were you, I would find a different job.

Notice that 'I' is followed by 'were'. This is only possible in conditional sentences.

Complete the following second conditional sentences.

   6 If governments destroyed all nuclear weapons, …

   7 If people didn't use money, …

   8 If the polar ice caps melted, …

   9 If I were president, …

   10 If I saw a ghost, …

Modals

Modal verbs include: must, have to, should, don't have to, mustn't, should, shouldn't, could, couldn't, can, can't, would, wouldn't, will and won't.
   In a sentence they always come after the subject and before a verb in the infinitive without 'to'.

Example
   I *might* go on holiday after the IELTS Test.
   New laws *must* be made to control pollution.

EXERCISE 30

Look at the following essay and put the correct modal verbs into the spaces. Sometimes there may be more than one possible answer.

Time target – 5 minutes

> *Women will play an increasingly important role in the work place of the future.*
>
> To what extent do you agree with the above?

In developed countries, recent trends suggest that in years to come women **(1)** _____ make up a large percentage of the workforce. There are a number of possible reasons for this.

Due to the recession in the developed world, companies are reluctant to take on full-time workers, who **(2)** _____ expect health care, a pension scheme and redundancy payments when dismissed. Instead, many employers prefer to hire people at an hourly rate. These employees tend to be women.

A lot of women (3) _____ commit themselves to a forty-hour week as they have children to look after. This is particularly true for single parent families, where the woman (4) _____ look after the children herself. There (5) _____ also be the perception that a woman is only working to supplement her husband's income and so full-time work is not as important.

It (6) _____ also be true to say that increasing sexual equality has meant that more women are reaching management positions. This in turn (7) _____ mean that the number of women also increases in lower positions, as women (8) _____ be keen to employ other women. If this is the case, this trend (9) _____ be expected to continue.

It seems likely that the number of working women (10) _____ continue to increase over the next few years as companies continue to seek a workforce that (11) _____ be easily dismissed and is more flexible in their working hours. Although this (12) _____ be a good thing in terms of sexual equality, it is a major setback in terms of worker rights.

Test Tips

Come prepared. Bring a pen, pencils, erasers and photo identification.

Reading

For any one reading:
- read all the questions first
- mark key words in the questions
- read the passage quickly, marking sections where you think answers to the questions are
- answer the questions by checking back and forth between the reading and the questions
- guess if you are not sure of the answer – do not leave any blanks.

Writing

For both tasks:
- do both tasks
- time yourself – 20 minutes for Task 1
- 40 minutes for Task 2
- plan before you write
- do the easiest task first
- try to leave enough time to check your grammar and spelling
- if you use words from the questions, spell them correctly
- remember – Task 1 asks for facts
- Task 2 asks for opinion.

EXERCISE 31

The answers to this quiz on the IELTS Test are in the Answer Key.

*Choose the appropriate letter **A–C** to answer the following questions.*

1 The Reading test consists of

    A a question booklet and a reading booklet

    B a reading booklet with four passages

    C a reading/question booklet and an answer sheet

2 The readings

    A each have their own specific types of questions

    B have between 38 and 42 questions each

    C become progressively more difficult

Decide if the following statements match the information given in this book by choosing:

YES [Y] *or*

NO [N] as appropriate.

3　You must not mark the question booklet in any way.

4　There are four main question types.

5　Multiple-choice questions always ask for specific information.

6　In the writing, you can do Task 2 first.

7　Questions can always be answered with a number or a letter of the alphabet.

Questions 8–10

Four *of the following statements* **A-H** *about the Writing test are true.*

Choose the **THREE** *letters for the remaining true statements and write them in the spaces below.*

8　.....................................

9　.....................................

10　.....................................

　　A　You should divide your time equally between the two tasks.

Example	*Answer*
B　There are two writing tasks. **[is true]**	**B**

　　C　Task 2 should be longer than Task 1.

　　D　Task 2 requires a description.

　　E　Evidence and examples are necessary in Task 2.

　　F　Task 2 requires a specialised discussion.

　　G　Task 1 is a business report.

　　H　In the writing, you can only get a good mark if you answer both questions.

Suggestions for Further Practice

The best practice you can get is to read in English as much as possible.

There are several IELTS practice books on the market and you can buy some of those. There are also many books available to help you increase your reading and writing skills in English. The following are particularly helpful in giving practice for the specific skills you will need for the IELTS.

Reading

Skilful Reading by Amy L. Sonka, published by Prentice–Hall, 1981.

Study Reading by Eric H. Glendinning and Beverly Holmström, published by Cambridge University Press, 1992.

Reading Skills for the Social Sciences by Louann Haarman, Patrick Leech and Janet Murray, published by Oxford University Press, 1988.

Writing

For Task 1: *Presenting Facts and Figures* by David Kerridge, published by Longmans, 1988.

For Task 2: *Essay Writing for English Tests* by Gabi Duigu, published by Academic Press, 1995.

Reading and Writing

Study Tasks in English by Mary Waters and Alan Waters, published by Cambridge University Press, 1995. If you are studying alone, you will also need to buy the Teacher's Book with this one.

Answer Key

Note: In the Answer Key the words in parentheses are optional. For example, 'radial (movement)' means your answer would be considered correct with or without the word 'movement'.

A slash indicates that any of the answers would be correct. For example, 'rock/soil' means that 'rock' is correct and 'soil' is correct. You only have to choose one of the words to be correct.

Section 1: Reading

IELTS PRACTICE TEST 1

There is no separate Answer Key for this test. You will find the answers as you work through the exercises in the book.

EXERCISE 1

A Polls Next Year

B Apec Delegate

C Church and State

D Cross-Strait Words

E Killings in Paris

F No to Tokyo

G Helping Hand

H Export Policy Attacked

I Labour Law Protest

J No Seats, No Support

K Risky Remarks

L Food Aid Short

EXERCISE 2

A **viii** ii and v both have the wrong focus. **ii** would require discussion of temperate fruit exports from other areas and v would require mention of other Chilean exports.

B **vi** ix suggests a description of a range of jobs in the fruit industry. It is too broad.

C **vii** only this one is possible.

D **i** this is broad enough to cover the whole paragraph. iv only covers the second half of the paragraph.

E **iii** the paragraph is not mainly about pesticides, so x would not be appropriate.

EXERCISE 3

1 **D** is the correct answer because the focus is on women in the paid labour force.

A is much too broad. For this answer to be correct there would have to be discussion of such issues as the legal position of women, their roles in the family and society, etc.

B only focuses on working **mothers**. The passage refers to women without children as well.

C is too broad with too wide a focus.

2 **C** is correct because it reflects the focus of this section.

A is much too broad. The section would have to include men in the labour force for this to be correct.

B This section does not mention either full- or part-time employment.

D only focuses on one sentence in the section.

3 **A** is correct because it reflects the focus of this section.

B focuses on only **one** benefit or gain.

C is not what the section is focused on. It is only one point in the section.

D also focuses on only one part of the section.

4 **B** reflects the general focus of this section.

A is much too broad and also implies the idea of physical threat which is not mentioned.

C refers only to the first paragraph of this section.

D is too broad and does not have the specific focus of B.

5 **B** reflects the main focus of this section.

A is only given as an example.

C is not what the section says.

D only focuses on the last sentence.

6 **C** covers the whole section.

A only focuses on women's wages.

B is mentioned, but is not the focus of the section.

D is only given as an example.

7 **A** reflects the main focus of this section.

B is only a comment on the **general perception** of women's roles and does not reflect the writer's point of view.

C focuses on only part of this section.

D This judgement does not reflect the focus of this section. The level of the tasks

women do (menial or otherwise) is not mentioned.

EXERCISE 4

1 Universal Salt Iodisation (USI). To find the answer, scan the section of the reading headed 'Iodine' for the year 1995 and read that sentence. You find that the question statement is a paraphrase of it.

2 & 3 Pakistan and Indonesia. Still in the section headed 'Iodine', scan for the names of two countries. It is easiest to scan for countries, because they begin with capital letters. When you find Pakistan and Indonesia, read that sentence which says 'salt iodisation was previously thought to be virtually impossible' which the question sentence paraphrases.

4 Technical monograph. Scan for the combination of these three capitalised acronyms. The answer is in the last paragraph on iodine.

5 **D** Scan the section headed 'Iodine' for the four capitalised words in quotation marks "Iodised Salt Support Facility" and read the part of the sentence which says 'the establishment of an 'Iodised Salt Support Facility' in Pakistan' and you have the answer.

6 **C** Scan for vitamin A in the section headed 'Vitamin A' and read a few words around each one you find. In the second paragraph you find 'fortification of sugar with vitamin A' and 'sugar fortification with vitamin A'. These give you the answer as it means vitamin A is added to sugar.

7 **B** As the questions in IELTS generally follow the order of the reading, for this question it is best to scan the remainder of the passage for the words 'fruit' and 'vegetables'. In the third paragraph of the section headed 'Vitamin A' you find 'fruits and vegetables'. The question sentence is a paraphrase of the sentence containing those words.

8 **A** Scan the rest of the passage for the words 'green revolution'. In the middle of the last paragraph you read 'the micro-nutrient content of foods had been neglected in the breeding of high yielding (green revolution) varieties of cereals such as rice.' 'Not taken fully into account' is another way of saying 'Had been neglected'. Always look for paraphrases of the question, rather than of the answer choices.

EXERCISE 5

1 professionals

2 clerks

3 labourers

4 formal training

5 training courses

6 work performance

7 technological change

8 quality assurance

[*Note that 7 & 8 can be in reverse order.*]

9 external [training] providers

EXERCISE 6

If you applied selective reading strategies here you would have realised that you did not need to read the first section of this reading. All the questions can be answered from the sections headed 'Sport and recreation particpation' and 'People who do not play sport'. You should have noticed that there is a reference in paren-theses to the relevant table at the end of each of these sections.

1	aerobics	4	no time/too busy
2	golf	5	bad weather
3	netball	6	no child care

EXERCISE 7   PART I

For the answers to Questions 1–6, you need to decide which answers are similar to the examples given in the reading. So you would decide that 'challenging assignments' is quite similar to 'achievement in the work', which is

a factor associated with the work and therefore associated with satisfaction. A 'pension plan', on the other hand, is associated with the 'working conditions' and is therefore more closely linked to dissatisfaction.

1	S	4	D
2	D	5	D
3	S	6	S

7 NO   The question statement reverses Herzberg's claim.

8 NOT GIVEN   Although it is stated that Herzberg conducted his research with accountants and engineers, there is no information given about the relevance of the theory to other professions.

9 NO   This contradicts the passage which says 'we must label Herzberg's theory as an intriguing but <u>unverified</u> framework …'

10 YES   This restates the section of the passage which says 'Some studies have found that job satisfaction and dissatisfaction were based on <u>different factors, and that these are in keeping with</u> the distinction made by Herzberg.'

11 NOT GIVEN   There is no information on **who** developed these strategies.

EXERCISE 7   PART II

12	B	16	MR
13	A	17	L
14	D	18	H
15	MR		

IELTS PRACTICE TEST 1: READING 1

1	C	8	NO
2	D	9	YES
3	B	10	YES
4	A	11	NOT GIVEN
5	C	12	YES
6	D	13	NO
7	NOT GIVEN		

1 NO This is the reverse of the first sentence in paragraph 1. Both statements compare the number of working women in Britain, Denmark and the EC, but the statement in the reading says that Britain has fewer economically active women than Denmark.

2 YES This summarised the whole of paragraph 2.

3 YES This is a rephrasing (a paraphrase) of the first sentence in paragraph 3.

4 NG There is no mention of women taking men's jobs in the reading.

5 YES This is a paraphrase of paragraph 3.

6 NO In paragraph 5 the writer indicates that industry should take advantage of women's skills developed in running a household. In fact, the question statement completely contradicts the main point of the writer's argument.

7 NO The reading does not say women are **unable** to contribute ideas. In fact it claims the opposite: that women have many ideas to contribute. It does claim that women do not have the opportunity to contribute their ideas because they are not fully a part of the organisation. So although the first part of the question sentence agrees with the writer, the second part contradicts him. Therefore, the answer is 'No'.

8 NG Whether women understand business strategy or not is never discussed in the reading. Therefore, the answer is 'Not given'.

9 NG Paragraph 7 gives details of the number of women presently in management and executive positions, but does not mention any changes to the situation. The use of 'more and more' in the question statement indicates a changing situation with the number of women in management increasing. Therefore, the answer is 'NG'.

10 NO In paragraph 8, the writer presents this as the 'stereotypical attitude', i.e. the view held by most people. The whole argument put forward by this writer contradicts this view. Therefore, this statement does not reflect the views of the writer.

11 YES This statement rephrases most of paragraphs 9 and 10.

12 C This is the thrust of the writer's argument. Therefore, C is the correct choice.

A The writer never expresses a view as to what kind of working behaviour is **appropriate for women**.

B In part this fits the stereotypical view which he mentions and argues against.

D The writer does mention that support programs are necessary to enable women to be more fully integrated in industry (paragraphs 9 and 10), but never suggests that these programs should necessarily be the responsibility of the government.

EXERCISE 9

1	Radial (movement)	11	NG
2	Horizontal (movement)	12	N
3	Vertical (movement)	13	V
4	Y	14	H
5	NG	15	R
6	NG	16	R
7	N	17	V
8	NG	18	V
9	NG	19	H
10	Y		

EXERCISE 10

1 provision
2 integration
3 providing
4 adopting
5 for long periods
6 to integrate

EXERCISE 11

1 expenditure
2 structured plan
3 job
4 work performance
5 employees
6 time
7 cost

EXERCISE 12

1 career change
2 hierarchy
3 fewer opportunities
4 job/work
5 retraining
6 work fulfilment
7 vertical movement/promotion
8 radial movement
9 power
10 influence
11 career growth

EXERCISE 13

1 gains
2 paid labour force
3 participation
4 informal labour sector
5 bargaining power
6 Furthermore
7 domestic

PRACTICE TEST 1: READING 3

26 remote/isolated (places)
27 forest (cover)
28 ore processing plant
29 solid sediment
30 dust, fumes (*must have both to be correct*)
31 (worthless) rock/soil
32 local population

33 voluntarily
34 themselves
35 power structure
36 disputes
37 authorities
38 impact
39 health and education

PRACTICE TEST 2

1 v
2 vi
3 ii
4 viii
5 iii
6 vii
7 O
8 N
9 N
10 B
11 O
12 *Melbourne Punch/Pix/People*
13 *Melbourne Punch*
14 *The Bulletin*
15 *Australasian Post*
16 *Penthouse/Playboy/Cleo/Cosmopolitan*
17 vii
18 viii
19 iv
20 ii
21 BR
22 N
23 AR
24 AR
25 N
26 B
27 individual cells
28 number of cells

29 damaged cells

30 offspring

31 germ cell

32 abnormalities

33 G

34 C

35 D

36 E

37 time/money/capital

38 radiation/nuclear accident

39 wind/sun/solar/hydro (*must have two to be correct*)

40 renewables/carbon-free energies

41 wind turbines/windmills

42 safely (and) cleanly

PRACTICE TEST 3

1	C	20	CO
2	B	21	SL
3	A	22	NL
4	D	23	Y
5	A	24	N
6	(small)gas turbine/	25	NG
	generator/(elastic)	26	NG
	steel chassis	27	N
7	plastic kits	28	Y
8	lighter	29	vii
9	GM	30	iii
10	R	31	vi
11	F	32	ii
12	R	33	ix
13	SC	34	C
14	R	35	G
15	B	36	A
16	A	37	F
17	D	38	D
18	C	39	B/E
19	PR		

Section 2: Writing

TASK 1

EXERCISE 1

1	world	9	retrenchment
2	land	10	gradual
3	harvested	11	grain
4	virgin	12	affected
5	program	13	government
6	great	14	policy
7	prices	15	market
8	rapid	16	forces

EXERCISE 2

1	past	7	rpd ↗ then ↘
2	# (number)	8	rpd ↗ then ↘
3	↗	9	grad then rpd ↗
4	↘	10	drmtc ↘
5	cont ↗	11	flctd
6	grad ↗		

EXERCISE 3 – SAMPLE ANSWERS

A From 1989 to 1995 the production of timber declined moderately.

B From 1986 to 1989 enrolment numbers decreased rapidly. Then, since 1989 to the present, enrolment numbers have increased steadily.

C From 1989 to 1995 Type I washing machine sales increased steadily, whereas Type II sales rose only slightly.

D From 1970 to 1975 LP sales increased slightly then decreased steadily to 1995. In contrast, cassette sales rose steadily from 1970 to 1995 and from 1985 CD sales grew rapidly.

EXERCISE 4

A From 1989 to 1995, there was a moderate decline in the production of timber.

B From 1986 to 1989, there was a rapid decrease in enrolment numbers. Then, from 1989 to now, there has been a steady increase in enrolment numbers.

C From 1989 to 1995 there was a steady increase in Type I washing machines sales, whereas there was a slight rise in Type II sales.

D From 1970 to 1975 there was a slight increase in LP sales, then there was a steady decrease to 1995. In contrast there was a steady rise in cassette sales from 1970 to 1995. From 1985, there was a steady growth in CD sales.

EXERCISE 5

1 exponential growth/dramatic increase
2 fluctuated
3 remained constant
4 upward trend
5 dropped dramatically

EXERCISE 6

1 of/to   6 to
2 at   7 at
3 by   8 by, of
4 at   9 at
5 at   10 at, to, at

EXERCISE 7

1 land
2 land area
3 insurance
4 the cost of insurance
5 the level of unemployment
6 unemployment levels
7 salaries

EXERCISE 8

This is a sample answer only.

From 1940 to 1960 the number of Indian and Pakistani immigrants increased slightly to just under 10 000 people. Then, after an initial drop, there was a rapid increase to over approximately 25 000 immigrants. Between 1965 and 1970 the number of immigrants fluctuated with an overall upward trend.

Similarly, the number of West Indian immigrants increased more moderately between 1940 and 1960 to roughly 15 000 people. Then there was a very sharp increase over a three-year period to a peak of just under 35 000 people. From 1963 to 1970 the number of immigrants dropped dramatically with some fluctuations to just over 5000 people.

[102 words]

EXERCISE 9

Time/tense	1994–past
Topic	♂:♀ arrsts + rsns why
General trend	arrst ♀ < ♂
Details	High % = Pblc drnkng ♂ = 32%, but ♀ > ♂; ♀ = 37%. ♀ > ♂ = Drnk drvng = 25%, Brch ordr = 17%, Theft = 16%, othr = 19% ♂ > ♀ = asslt = 18%
Conclusion	♀ arrstd < ♂ police don't arrst ♀ ?

EXERCISE 10

Here are some sample sentences for you to compare with your own.

A Theft is the most common crime.

Theft is slightly more common than violence.

Theft is just under four times more common than other crimes, excluding violence.

Aside from theft, there are three times more incidences of violence than of other crimes.

B Full-time employment is the most common type of employment.

Full-time employment is considerably more common than part-time and casual employment.

About twice as many people are employed in full-time work than in casual work.

EXERCISE 11

Incorporating data

Here are some sentences for you to compare with your own.

A Theft is the most common crime, with 94 cases per 10 000 people.

Theft, of which there are 94 cases per 10 000 people, is slightly more common than violence (65cases).

Theft, which accounts for 94 cases per 10 000 people, is just under 4 times more common than the other crimes (25 cases).

Not including theft, there are 3 times more cases of violence (94 cases per 10 000 people) than of other crimes (25 cases).

B Full-time employment, which makes up 56.18%, is the most common type of employment.

Full-time employment (56.18%) is considerably more common than part-time (19.24%) and casual employment (24.58%).

About twice as many people are employed in full-time work (just over 50%) than in casual work, which accounts for about 25%.

EXERCISE 12

Here is a sample answer describing the charts.

The two pie charts show the proportion of males and females arrested and the bar chart shows reasons why they were arrested.

In general females were arrested much less frequently than males and were arrested mostly for public drinking and assault, whereas males were more likely to be arrested for a range of other crimes.

The pie chart shows that about one third of the male population was arrested in 1994, while only nine per cent of the female population was arrested. The highest percentage of arrests of men, which was approximately 32%, was for public drinking. However, this percentage was less than the percentage of females arrested for the same reason, which was approximately 37%. Males were more commonly arrested for drink driving, which constituted just over 25%, breach of order (about 17%), other crimes (approximately 17%) and theft (16%). Other offences in which females were more commonly arrested than males were for assault, where it constituted just under 18% of the arrests. Five per cent of men and about 6.5% of women refused to say why they were arrested.

It appears that women are either more law-abiding than men or that law enforcement officers are more reluctant to arrest women.

[200 words]

EXERCISE 13

There are no sample answers for this exercise.

EXERCISE 14

One way to do this exercise is to group the sports according to team sports and individual sports and then describe the most and least popular in each.

Team sports: rugby, football, cricket, baseball

Individual sports: swimming, athletics, golf, tennis

EXERCISE 15: SAMPLE ANSWER

The table shows the differences in salaries for males and females for several jobs at the National Institute of Health (NIH).

As can be seen, men's salaries exceed those of women in all positions except for one job type. There are also many more males employed at the NIH than females.

It is clear that females at the NIH earn significantly less money than males with differences in salaries ranging between $197 and $9121. For example, a male investigator with a PhD earns $67 131 whereas a female in the same position earns $61 164. It is only in the position of Lab Chief MD where salaries for females are higher (by $10 509). However, it must be noted that there are only seven women in this position.

There are 483 males with MD qualifications compared to just 71 females. Similarly there are 473 male employees who have a PhD whereas there are only 118 women. The biggest difference in numbers for any one position is in the position of investigator with a PhD. There are 251 males and only 85 females.

In summary, it is clear that there is little equity between the sexes at the NIH in terms of salary and numbers of each sex employed.

[183 words]

EXERCISE 16: SAMPLE ANSWER

The chart shows what administrative procedures are carried out from when the examination is completed to when the marks are sent to the candidate.

The reading and listening tests are collected and marked by the administrator. The administrator then retains the marks and waits for the other test scores to come in.

The speaking test is assessed by the examiner. Then the marks are sent to the administrator. The interview tape is then sent to the examination board where the tape is either reassessed or stored. The writing test is marked by another examiner and the marks are sent to the administrator. Similarly, the writing test paper is sent to the examination board for further reassessment or storage.

Once the marks have been collected by the administrator and the overall band score calculated, a certificate is made out and sent to the candidate.

[142 words]

TASK 2

Note that most of the answers given here are only samples. There are generally many other possibilities.

EXERCISE 17

1 Should animals be used to test the safety of new products?

2 Should the ownership of private cars be taxed very heavily to subsidise cheap or free rail travel?

3 Is the government responsible for providing high-quality free health care for the people?

EXERCISE 18

1 Should women give up their jobs to reduce unemployment?

2 Would women returning to the role of housewife improve moral values?

3 Do you agree that women will play an increasingly important role in the workplace?

EXERCISE 19

For	Against
World-wide communication possible	Only the rich can afford access to the internet
Greater access to information	Computing skills are necessary to operate the internet, so a new technology gap develops
Makes copyright laws harder to enforce, so harder to keep new technology secret	
Difficult to censor	

EXERCISE 20

1   As public safety is of the highest importance, it is often necessary to test new products on animals. It is better for a few animals to suffer than for human life to be placed at risk by untested products.

For	Against
Realistic tests are necessary	Not all animal tests are important
Better that animals suffer than humans	Animals have rights
Tests are necessary to find cures	Often computer simulation is possible

2   If countries are serious about solving traffic problems, they should tax private cars very heavily and use the money to provide free or very cheap rail travel.

For	Against
Taxes on cars would discourage people from using cars	No door-to-door service
	Unpopular with car owners so a vote loser
Good public transport would increase the mobility of the people	Takes time to develop the infrastructure
Save natural resources	

3   The quality of health care a person receives should not depend on the size of their bank balance. The government is responsible for providing a high level of health care for all its citizens.

For	Against
Health is a fundamental right	Health is the responsibility of the individual
Good hospitals are governmental responsibility	Ageing population makes health care impractical
A healthy population is vital to national interests	

EXERCISE 21

Although it is definitely true that a government is responsible for protecting its people, it is less certain that spending money on defence is the best way to do this. Some countries, for example Costa Rica, spend virtually nothing on defence and yet manage to survive. It would therefore be true to say there are ways of protecting people that do not necessitate a vast military build-up.

EXERCISE 22

1   Nobody should marry before the age of 30.

For

People who marry after the age of 30 have had an opportunity to see a bit of the world and are more likely to know the full implications of married life. Many people who marry young end up getting divorced because they are not experienced enough to deal with the unfamiliar set of problems that married life inevitably brings.

Against

It is an overgeneralisation to say that nobody should marry before they are 30. People are different and so some people may be ready to marry very young, whereas other people might still not be ready to marry at 30. Besides, one of the main reasons for marriage is to have children and too large an age gap between generations can cause cause relationship difficulties later.

2   Everybody has the right to carry a gun.

For

One of the fundamental rights of humankind is to protect him- or herself. Therefore the government has no right to tell people that they can't carry a gun. A gun is not dangerous in itself, it is the person who uses it who is dangerous, so rather than ban weapons, it is more sensible to educate people to use weapons responsibly.

Against

If people are allowed to carry guns, they will use them. Therefore the easier it is to buy a gun, the higher the number of people who will get shot. It is noticeable how much higher the murder rate is in America, where guns are allowed, compared to Britain where guns are not. To allow people to own guns only serves to escalate the amount of violence that is tolerated.

3   Patriotism is the biggest cause of war.

For

Patriotism teaches people to believe that your country, and by implication your government, is always right. This makes it easy for unscrupulous politicians to manipulate the pride the patriot feels in his or her country to hatred of other countries seen as rivals or enemies.

Against

It is very important for people to feel pride in their country. When people are patriotic they are more likely to take an interest in the country's day-to-day running and therefore less likely to allow unscrupulous politicians to drive a country to war.

EXERCISE 23

Although taxing private cars would be an unpopular short-term measure, it would eventually solve the problem of road congestion. Cheap railways and expensive cars are undoubtedly in the public interest. However, it is unlikely that any government has the political will necessary to bring in measures which would undoubtedly alienate influential groups within society.

EXERCISE 24

1   There are three main reasons why I don't like going to Capunk.

2   If managers are to be successful, they need to motivate their staff.

3   There is enough food in the world to feed everybody.

EXERCISE 25

1   **Watching too much television reduces people's capacity to think for themselves.** Firstly, watching television makes people lazy as viewers are given second-hand opinions, which can be used as a substitute for individual thought. Secondly, most television programmes are primarily entertainment as they are designed to attract viewers away from rival channels. Therefore they are aimed to appeal to the lowest common denominator and have little educational value. Unlike books or even radio, television leaves little scope for the imagination and so tends to dictate simplified role models of what life should be like.

2 If people are allowed to carry guns the number of murders will increase. The link between guns and murders has been consistently proved by world crime figures. There are more people murdered in America than in Europe, largely because guns are readily available. It stands to reason that if people can easily obtain guns, they will use them. Therefore the only way to control gun-related crime is to make it extremely difficult for ordinary people to own a gun.

EXERCISE 26

1 She found lipstick on his shirt so she left him.

2 He woke up because someone was throwing stones at the window.

3 I came to the lesson late so I missed the test.

4 Rainforests are important to the environment as they act as the lungs of the world.

5 Unleaded petrol reduces exhaust emissions because it reduces the amount of toxic gases in the atmosphere.

6 Most people in prison come from poor social backgrounds. Therefore they have no opportunity to engage a good lawyer.

EXERCISE 27

1 Most countries have made some efforts to control the traffic in their major cities. However, these efforts have often failed, because the number of cars increases so rapidly that the measures taken are immediately out of date.

2 Floods are a major problem in the city but the government seems to be making very little effort to improve the situation. Although they often make speeches about the importance of water catchment areas, they continue to build on every available green space.

3 Many people say the space program is a waste of money but developing another planet could be the answer to overpopulation. Although life may be possible on another planet, it would probably not be very pleasant.

4 Rainforests are a valuable source of biodiversity and new drugs. However, they could also be used to feed the poor and provide them with farm land. Although trees are useful for stopping erosion, logging companies provide jobs and wood product exports are a valuable source of foreign exchange.

EXERCISE 28

The correct forms of the verbs are in brackets following the underlined error.

Over the past 30 years, many countries have spent most of their income repaying the interest on foreign debts. Many people <u>are consider</u> (consider) the initial loans responsible for these debts to be more beneficial to the lender than to the borrower.

In the past, most developing countries were short of ready funds to build the infrastructure necessary for development. Therefore, foreign countries were asked to provide loans for projects to help the countries <u>will become</u> (become) self reliant. However, this money <u>often to be used</u> (was often used) to make quick profits for developers or to line the pockets of corrupt officials. Once the money is used the problem of repayment <u>had began</u> (begins).

Since the 1970s many developing countries have found that they can't pay back the loans or even the interest <u>is accumulate</u> (accumulated) on the loans. Consequently the countries have borrowed more money to pay back the interest. This gave western countries the power <u>dictates</u> (to dictate) government policy through the World Bank and the International Monetary Fund. These financial institutions <u>only interest</u> (are only interested) in balance sheets. Therefore nations <u>forced</u> (have been forced) to adopt policies which do nothing to develop their resources or improve the lives of the local people.

Countries that get caught in this debt spiral <u>had</u> (have) no chance of paying back the initial money borrowed, while the banks making the loans make two or three times the money lent after the interest payments are taken into account. As most donor countries <u>were already repaid</u> (have already been repaid), both in terms of money and in terms of economic interest, it is morally right for developing countries to refuse to pay back foreign loans.

EXERCISE 29

1   If the world population continues to increase, many people will starve.

2   If the number of cars isn't controlled, traffic jams will get worse.

3   If it rains this afternoon, it will be difficult to get home.

4   If I get a band eight in the IELTS Test, I will have a party.

5   If there is life on another planet, they may be trying to make contact.

6   If governments destroyed all nuclear weapons, people would feel much safer.

7   If people didn't use money, they would have to use a barter system.

8   If the polar ice caps melted, many countries would be flooded.

9   If I were president, I would make Monday a holiday.

10   If I saw a ghost, I would try and take a photograph.

EXERCISE 30

1	will	7	might/may
2	would	8	can
3	cannot (can't)	9	can
4	has to	10	will
5	might/may	11	can
6	may/might	12	may/might/could

EXERCISE 31

1	C	6	YES
2	C	7	NO
3	NO	8	C
4	YES	9	E
5	NO	10	H

Acknowledgments

The authors would like to thank Geoffrey Crewes and Richard Howells for their support in this project.

The authors and publishers wish to thank copyright holders for granting permission to reproduce illustrative material and textual extracts. Sources are as follows:

Jonathan Agranoff for his article 'Religious dentistry'; Australian Government Publishing Service for the extracts from 'Training', 'Sport and recreation' and the table 'Number of dwellings by State/Territory, 1994' all taken from *Year Book Australia 1996*, Australian Bureau of Statistics: Commonwealth of Australia, Copyright reproduced by permission; *The Ecologist*, (Agriculture House, Bath Road, Sturminster Newton, Dorset DT10 1DU, England) for the extract from *The Ecologist*, Vol. 26, No. 4, July/August 1996, and the extract from 'A woman's work is never done', *The Ecologist*, Vol. 26, No. 4, July/August 1996; *The Economist* for the article 'Asia's energy temptation', 7 October 1995, for the extracts from 'New age transport', 25 December 1993–7 January 1994, and the tables 'Consumer goods' and Televisions' from 13 April 1996, (c) *The Economist*, London; *Far Eastern Economic Review* for extracts from 'Regional briefing', 22 August, 31 October, 7, 14, 21 November, 5 December, No. 3, 1994; Gower Publishing Company for the table 'Date of entry to the UK', taken from *Britain's Black Population* by the Runnymeade Trust and the Radical Statistics Race Group; Heinemann Educational, 1980; Virginia Jackson for extracts from her article 'Domestic pets in new urban areas', from *Australian Planner*, Vol. 31, No. 3, 1994; Liverpool University Press for extracts from 'Viewpoint: Do we need cities any more?' by Ian Davison, *Town Planning Review*, Vol. 66, No. 1, January 1995; MAC MacDonald Communications Corporation for the extracts from the article 'Getting girls on-line', which first appeared in *Working Woman* in April 1994. Written by Katie Hafner. Reprinted with the permission of MacDonald Communications Corporation. (c) 1994 by MacDonald Communications Corporation. For subscriptions call 1-800-234-9675; MCB University Press for extracts from 'Utilising women's skills' by Sam Thomason, *Employment Bulletin and Industrial Relations Digest*, Vol. 7, No. 4, 1991; The Open University for the tables 'Working patterns of mothers with young children' taken from R. Bocock and K. Thompson, *Social and Cultural Forms of Modernity*, Open University and Polity Press, 1992; Prentice Hall, UK, for extracts from 'Theories of job satisfaction' and the extract and graphs from 'The changing nature of careers', *Behaviour in Organisations: Understanding and Managing the Human Side of Work*, Fifth Edition, Jerald Green and Robert A. Baron, Prentice Hall International Editions; *Science* for the table 'Pay of NIH scientists by gender', taken from *Science*, Vol. 260, 14 May 1993; Simon and Schuster International Group for the table 'Quality of life in five countries', from Joseph Weatherby *et al.*, *The Other World: Issues and Politics in the Third World*, Macmillan (New York), 1986; The United Nations Subcommittee on Nutrition for the extract from 'Micronutrients', SCN News, No. 13, 1995; Lindsay Vane for the extract from *The Way We Were*, Lindsay Vane, OUP, 1983; W. W. Norton & Company for the table 'World grain harvested area, 1950–96' from Bowen, Kane & Roodman, *Vital Signs*, Washington DC: World Watch Institute, 1994.

Every effort has been made to trace the original source of copyright material contained in this book. The publisher would be pleased to hear from copyright holders to rectify any errors or omissions.

IELTS Reading Answer Sheet

Module taken:

Academic ☐   General Training ☐

Version number:
Please enter the number in the boxes and shade the number in the grid

00	10	20	30	40	50	60	70	80	90
☐	☐	☐	☐	☐	☐	☐	☐	☐	☐

0	1	2	3	4	5	6	7	8	9
☐	☐	☐	☐	☐	☐	☐	☐	☐	☐

#		✓ ✗		#		✓ ✗
1		☐☐		31		☐☐
2		☐☐		32		☐☐
3		☐☐		33		☐☐
4		☐☐		34		☐☐
5		☐☐		35		☐☐
6		☐☐		36		☐☐
7		☐☐		37		☐☐
8		☐☐		38		☐☐
9		☐☐		39		☐☐
10		☐☐		40		☐☐
11		☐☐		41		☐☐
12		☐☐		42		☐☐
13		☐☐				
14		☐☐				
15		☐☐				
16		☐☐				
17		☐☐				
18		☐☐				
19		☐☐				
20		☐☐				
21		☐☐				
22		☐☐				
23		☐☐				
24		☐☐				
25		☐☐				
26		☐☐				
27		☐☐				
28		☐☐				
29		☐☐				
30		☐☐				

Band Score		Reading Total	